The Wyrdest Link

D1628015

Also by David Langford in Gollancz:

THE UNSEEN UNIVERSITY CHALLENGE

The Wyrdest Link

The Second Discworld® Quizbook

DAVID LANGFORD

Copyright © 2002 David Langford

All rights reserved

The right of David Langford to be identified as the
author of this work has been asserted by him in accordance
with the Copyright, Designs and Patents Act 1988.

Discworld ® is a trade mark registered by Terry Pratchett

This edition first published in Great Britain in 2002 by
Victor Gollancz Ltd
A subsidiary of the Orion Publishing Group
Orion House, 5 Upper St Martin's Lane,
London WC2H 9EA

A CIP catalogue record for this book
is available from the British Library

ISBN 0 575 07319 5

Set in Plantin Light by
Deltatype Ltd, Birkenhead, Merseyside

Printed in Great Britain by
Clays Ltd, St Ives plc

This one was always going to be for my favourite aunt, Louise, who encouraged the infant Langford to read that crazy science fiction stuff. She enjoyed life enormously, always brightened it for others, and deserved more of it herself.

Also for Josh Kirby (1928–2001), first and greatest Discworld artist, who sadly died on the day this book was delivered. *The Wyrdest Link* was his last Discworld cover painting.

In fond memory:
Louise Talbott (*née* Pearse),
29 April 1941 to 9 October 2001

David Langford was born in 1953, took an honours degree in physics at Brasenose College, Oxford, worked for several years as a nuclear weapons physicist with the Ministry of Defence, and since 1980 has been a freelance author and editor. He is married, with a happy absence of children, and lives in Reading, Berkshire.

His published books include *War in 2080: The Future of Military Technology* (nonfiction), *An Account of a Meeting with Denizens of Another World, 1871* (non-fact UFO spoof), *The Space Eater* (a science fiction novel), *The Leaky Establishment* (comedy about nuclear weaponry, reissued in 2001 with an appreciative introduction by Terry Pratchett), *Earthdoom!* (farcical disaster novel written with John Grant), *The Dragonhiker's Guide to Battlefield Covenant at Dune's Edge: Odyssey Two* (SF parody collection), *The Silence of the Langford* (articles, essays and speeches), and *The Complete Critical Assembly* (book reviews). A fuller list appears on his website at www.ansible.demon.co.uk.

Langford has received many awards for his writing and SF journalism, including the British SF Association Award for short fiction and – twenty times as of 2001 – science fiction's top prize, the Hugo Award.

His association with Terry Pratchett goes back to the early years of Discworld. In 1985 he described *The Colour of Magic* in his regular *White Dwarf* book review column as 'one of those horrible, antisocial books which impel the reader to buttonhole friends and quote bits at them.' As a freelance editor, Langford wrote the reader's report recommending the publication of *Equal Rites*, and has worked on almost all the full-length Discworld novels since the fourth, *Mort*. As a contributor to reference books, he has analysed Pratchett in David Pringle's *St James Guide to Fantasy* and *The Ultimate Encyclopedia of Fantasy*, in the multiple award-winning *The Encyclopedia of Fantasy* ed. John Clute and John Grant, in his text commentary for Josh Kirby's art book *A Cosmic Cornucopia*, and in an introduction to the millennial collection of academic studies *Terry Pratchett: Guilty of Literature* ed. Andrew M. Butler, Edward James and Farah Mendlesohn.

Langford had probably been fated to write the first official Discworld quizbook *The Unseen University Challenge* (1996) ever since the 1980s conversation in which he said, '*I* know where the name Rincewind comes from . . .' and Terry Pratchett replied: 'You bastard!' Now the inquisition continues in *The Wyrdest Link*.

Introduction by Terry Pratchett

Not long ago a newspaper, in one of those nice articles newspapers occasionally write to tell people who this Terry Pratchett person is, used the sentence: 'He steals blatantly'. In an article about Another Author, the phrase used was: 'draws gloriously on ancient and modern cultural references'. Both journalists meant the same thing, but I couldn't help wondering what would have happened if the phrases had been swopped around, and where the wreckage would have landed.

Research (for it is that of which we speak, thank you so very much) tends to happen by itself, if you've got your mind right. In the past year or two I've *knowingly* researched chimney sweeping, chocolate, clock-making and rats, but God alone know what else I've picked up. The best research takes place when you think you're doing something else, when information piles up in the attics of the brain and over time ceases to become words you have read and becomes things you can't remember ever not knowing. Like volvas – they were Nordic seeresses (very safe ones, possibly, with riding lights) who wore catskin hoods and gloves. Or that Niflheim, a sort of Nordic hell, is very dreary and cold, and therefore instantly became Sniflheim to me the moment I read about it, which was probably when I was thirteen and would read anything if I thought it might have runes in it.

Research is reading, for interest, a book with a multi-typeface title so long that there's a small lay-by halfway though it where soft drinks may be purchased: The 1864 'Cyclopedia of Commercial and Business ANECDOTES comprising INTERESTING REMINISCENCES AND FACTS, Remarkable Traits & Humours, AND Notable Sayings, Dealings, Experiences and Witticisms of MERCHANTS, TRADERS,

BANKERS, MERCANTILE CELEBRITIES, MILLION-AIRES, BARGAIN MAKERS, etc, etc . . .' and let's stop there for a Vimto, with *half the title still to go*. But the research there isn't in picking up occasional nuggets of fact to win a round of Trivial Pursuit, it's in getting the sense of the world view of men for whom money wasn't a thing but a process. And the feel of a world where you could have titles like that.

Do this for long enough and you end up getting an education, or something that passes for one in poor lighting conditions.

Discworld is full of the results. As Dave Langford points out, some of the weirdest things in Discworld are simpy obscure by-ways of the history of our planet. If you want to see a fantasy world, open your eyes and step outside.

It's worrying for me to read this book. I have to research Discworld now, mindful of the fact that some throw-away line in *The Light Fantastic* might prevent a whole wonderful plot happening twenty books down the line (thank goodness for quantum interpretations of time). So much has happened – and, with luck, still remains to happen. It's a frightening thought. If I'd known Discworld would be this popular, I'd have written better books . . .

Terry Pratchett

Read This Now

Once upon a time in 1996 there was *The Unseen University Challenge*, a Discworld quizbook loosely organized as a collection of eighty-odd tricky test papers from Unseen University, the legendary wizards' college of Terry Pratchett's Discworld. Now, in the same brain-warping tradition, we have *The Wyrdest Link*. Unbearable humiliations await the rash contender!

This time, the quiz themes come from Discworld's many guilds, societies and organizations, from long-established ones like the Thieves' and Assassins' Guilds (found near the opening of the very first Discworld book) to others that came to prominence much later, like the Accountants. Additional featured groups include the eight orders of wizardry, the Ankh-Morpork City Watch and even the Librarians of Time and Space.

When that first quizbook was completed there were a mere eighteen Discworld novels about which to pose smartarse questions, from *The Colour of Magic* in 1983 to *Maskerade* in 1996, plus a handful of spinoffs like comic-book adaptations and *The Discworld Companion*. Further novels drawn on for *The Wyrdest Link* begin with *Feet of Clay* in 1996, continuing through *Hogfather*, *Jingo*, *The Last Continent*, *Carpe Jugulum* and *The Truth*, until we reach *Thief of Time* and *The Last Hero*, both published in 2001 and bringing the official count to twenty-seven.

But of course it's not that simple: this count ignores *The Science of Discworld*, whose fictional strand is a canonical Discworld story comparable in length to *Eric* or *The Last Hero*, but which didn't appear from either of Terry Pratchett's usual publishers. Incidentally, *The Science of Discworld* provides the useful term 'Roundworld' to distinguish our own non-discoid Earth: this is used freely and gratefully in *The Wyrdest Link*.

As before, the main focus is on book-length Discworld fiction – although shorter works and the countless spinoffs like

Mappes, Diaries, Portfolios and the like do get an occasional mention. There are, thank heaven, no questions about Discworld computer games. Well . . . perhaps just one.

As before, you are warned that it really would be quite a good idea to have read a lot of Discworld novels before tackling this challenge, at least if you don't want to be told rather rudely: 'You Are The Wyrdest Link.' On the other hand, being able to answer most or all of the questions off the top of your head does suggest excessive devotion and the need to get out more.

Additionally, it's useful to have what Terry Pratchett calls a broad but shallow knowledge of eccentric trivia about our own world, since Discworld – world and mirror of worlds – is full to bursting with little jokes and allusions that reflect earthly doings, preferably weird ones. The daftest things in Discworld can sometimes be unsparingly accurate depictions of Round-world quirks. You have been warned.

The quizmaster has learned a certain amount from constructive feedback, abuse, and death threats in the wake of *The Unseen University Challenge*, and has tried to avoid questions which turn on excessively minute knowledge of excessively minor Discworld characters, or are otherwise too bloody perverse and difficult. Well, perhaps just a *few* of the latter.

As before, there are guaranteed to be no boring old acrostics, 'how many names can you find . . .' letter squares, or Discworld anagrams. Well, just one for those who insist: WILD SCROD.

By special request of our publishers, the **Answers** appear at the back of the book rather than following each quiz, and begin on page 93. Each set of answers includes a follow-on question giving you a chance to score a bonus point in the **Extra Answers**, beginning on page 197. To make life simpler, the vast Hints section in *The Unseen University Challenge* has been abolished and occasional hints built into questions instead.

Finally, a unique offer: fill in all the answers in your copy of *The Wyrdest Link*, mail it by registered post to yourself, and you will be automatically entered in our prize competition. Every winner will receive a personalized copy of *The Wyrdest Link* with the answers filled in. Perhaps even correctly.

So . . . *are* you the Wyrdest Link? Read on, and begin to find out.

David Langford

Questions

PROTEGO ET SERVIO

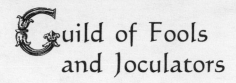

Guild of Fools and Joculators

An easy quiz to begin with! Naturally the Fools must stay in character by asking foolishly easy questions, but also insist on their own tomfool answers. Score a point for getting either the Fool or the Non-Fool answer ... (**Answers** on page 95.)

1 Which, numerically, was the Discworld novel that introduced Granny Weatherwax?

2 Which wizard was born under the Small Boring Group of Faint Stars?

3 What was the sticky basis of the glue invented by Leonard of Quirm for the Discworld equivalent of Post-It Notes?

4 Which Archchancellor of Unseen University shared a surname with a noted witch, a distant cousin whom he never met?

5 What austere ingredients were cooked up for Hogswatch dinner by one of Ankh-Morpork's poshest restaurants when the food vanished?

6 What was the single question on the world's easiest examination paper?

7 Which High Priest of the Sun reckoned it was a blessing he had the looks for the job: 'a tall frame, a bald head and a nose you could plough rocks with'?

8 What is the inevitable name of the longest uncurved street in Discworld's greatest city?

9 Which glamorous canine was characterized by Gaspode the Wonder Dog as having the brains of a stunned herring?

10 In which novel does the City Watch's latest recruit identify his duties as 'To Serve The Public Trust, Protect The Innocent, And Seriously Prod Buttock'?

The Lancre Witches

Witches, of course have no organization and no leaders. It's just that particular respect is given to some of the leaders they don't have. (**Answers** on page 97.)

1 What is the usual verdict in the Lancre Witch Trials?

2 Which witch read the future in a bowl of jambalaya?

3 Which witch brooded on the saying that inside every fat girl was a thin girl and a lot of chocolate, and even knew the name of her thin girl?

4 Which witch, for about three or four hours when young, used the utterly cool name Endemonidia?

5 Which witch was summoned three times to the same childbirth?

6 Which witch inherited the uncharacteristic role of fairy godmother?

7 What did Nanny Annaple have in profusion that made even top witch Granny Weatherwax deeply envious?

8 What terrible though rarely performed ritual, involving Nanny Ogg, several kettles and a banjo, spread panic through the village?

9 It wasn't over until . . . which witch sang?

10 Which witch caused outrage by 'standin' there bifurcated' so that people could see where her legs were?

Offler's League of Temperance

Discworld offers a variety of fascinating beverages, not all of them soft drinks. Here are ten to test your palate and dissolve your teeth. (**Answers** on page 98.)

1 Who drank one of those special cocktails of layered, multicoloured liquors containing vegetation, paper umbrellas and ice cubes in the shape of little elephants?

2 What 'very fine' product carries the surname of its maker Jimkin Bearhugger?

3 'You don't like brandy, dear. You like your special oat drink with the vitamins,' said the wife of – which horseman?

4 What tipple favoured by vampires on the wagon is also a Hungarian wine known locally as Bikavér?

5 What's unusual about the hangover produced by wine made from reannual grapes?

6 What is the only drink available in the office of Mr Slant the lawyer?

7 Which Guild leader's tantalus held bottles labelled Mur, Nig, Trop and Yksihw?

8 What would you make from the Lancre Blackheart, the Golden Disagreeable or the Green Billet?

9 What was the brown, viscous froth oozing from every door and window of the shop, piling up in mounds that almost hid it?

10 When Igor at the undead bar was asked for one of these, 'he didn't mix a metaphor' – what's the drink?

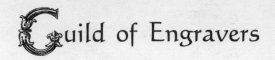

Guild of Engravers

Until certain developments in a later Discworld novel, printing with movable type was prohibited in Ankh-Morpork and messages to be printed in multiple copies were hand-carved into wooden blocks by Guild members. Which books featured the following inscriptions or signs, not necessarily engraved? (**Answers** on page 99.)

1 NEITHER RAIN NOR SNOW NOR GLOM OF NIT ...

2 MALIGNITY.

3 A Storie of Forbiden Love! A Searing Sarger of Passion that Bridged Spaes and Tyme! Thys wille shok you!

4 KLATCHIAN HOT REVUE ... HOYDENS! HOYDENS! HOYDENS!

5 Do Not Put Your Neck On This Block.

6 GOOD NEWS! Om Welcomes You!!!

7 Will Threaten For Food.

8 One Sun Mirror.

9 IGNORE THIS SIGN. By Order.

10 (On the wizards' map of Ankh-Morpork:) Here be Dragons.

Minor Guilds and Societies

Some Discworld organizations have died out or failed as yet to achieve lasting prominence. Let us salute them in their obscurity. (**Answers** on page 100.)

1 The League Against Cruelty to Dogs announced itself with much-dribbled-on notes pushed under the ruler's door: 'DeER Cur, The CruELt to HOMLIss DoGs In thIs CITy Is A DIssGrays ...' Who is believed responsible?

2 Which society's final meeting began with the question, 'Are the Cups of Integrity well and truly suffused?'

3 Which society sent in a terminally dull report of a meeting where they argued for two hours about changes in the show rules for parrots?

4 On what fraught occasion of industrial action was the Guild of Watchmen formed?

5 What was the sole recorded achievement of Lancre's Royal Society for the Betterment of Mankind, for which the King awarded Shawn Ogg a small medal?

6 What did members of the Guild of Handlemen actually do? (Whips are involved.)

7 Complete the musical signature of the Guild of Barber-Surgeons: 'shave and a haircut ...'

8 With which Guild are Ludd's Lads and Lasses associated?

9 Which ethical Ankh-Morpork minority took over the duties of the outlawed Guild of Firefighters, which frankly had been little more than a protection racket?

10 Where do we learn of the Guild of Science Writers and its ironclad rules that texts must mention cats locked in boxes, torches shone from fast-moving vehicles, and the Trousers of Time?

The Librarians of Time and Space

It is well known to Librarians that all libraries, everywhere and everywhen, are linked by the esoteric pathways and inexplicable plot convenience of L-Space. In particular, there are connections between Discworld and the strange other place known as Roundworld or Earth ... (**Answers** on page 101.)

1 What does Roundworld author Evelyn Waugh have to do with the City Watch adventure in which Ankh-Morpork is terrorized by a gonne?

2 Which Discworld novel title comes from a music-hall verse by the otherwise forgotten G.W. Hunt (died 1904), beginning 'We don't want to fight ...' and ending 'The Russians shall not have Constantinople'?

3 Roundworld author Christopher Priest published an SF novel called *A Dream of Wessex* (hideously retitled *The Perfect Lover* in America), whose original working title was vetoed by his publishers as insufficiently interesting. Some time later it became the title of a Discworld novel – which?

4 A certain Roundworld director of music was made famously infamous in the play and movie *Amadeus*. Can you link him by name to his Discworld equivalent?

5 What was most improbably photographed in Rudyard Kipling's supernatural story 'At the End of the Passage', and again in *Feet of Clay*?

6 Which Roundworld city provided the inspiration for Ankh-Morpork's underground chaos of abandoned, built-over streets?

7 In *The Last Continent* there are problems in naming a fruity dessert after the great but unfortunately surnamed singer Dame Nellie Butt – echoing which Roundworld dish?

8 Which novice of the History Monks sounds like a personage from whom, under the right circumstances, one should claim five pounds?

9 What's the hidden connection or paper trail between the arsenic poisoning attempt on the Patrician in *Feet of Clay*, and the death of Napoleon Bonaparte?

10 What does Roundworld author Leslie Charteris have to do with the illustrated Discworld saga in which Cohen the Barbarian plans to return fire to the gods?

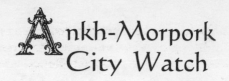

Ankh-Morpork City Watch

The City Watch is always – well, almost always – alert for suspicious behaviour, and its men are highly trained to spot anomalies. So which is the odd one out in each of these lists? (**Answers** on page 103.)

1 Artistically: *The Discworld Companion, Feet of Clay, Mort: a Discworld Big Comic, The Streets of Ankh-Morpork, The Unseen University Challenge.*

2 Elementally: bursarium, cohenium, runium, wranglium.

3 Experimentally: Mad Doctor Scoop, Psychoneurotic Lord Snapcase, Crazed Baron Haha, Screaming Doctor Berserk, Dribbling Doctor Vibes.

4 Geographically: Bad Heisses Bad, Bad Schüschein, Bes Pelargic, Bonk, Bugs.

5 Inundatingly: bedsteads, chocolate biscuits, fish, frogs, sardines (tinned), shrimp.

6 Martially: déjà-fu, no kando, okidoki, puzuma, shiitake, upsidazi.

7 Regionally: clootie dumplings, slumpie, squishi, Distressed Pudding, Jammy Devils.

8 Spontaneously: Cheerful Fairy, Eater of Socks, Dragon of Unhappiness, Hair Loss Fairy, Verruca Gnome.

9 Vitally: Mr Slant, Windle Poons (after half-past nine), Count de Magpyr, Reg Shoe, Baron Saturday.

10 Wondrously: hard pad, soft pad, the swinge, slab throat, scroff, mange.

Philosopher's Tavern

The philosophers of Ephebe are able to cope with advanced symbolic logic, but we're letting you off with an easy example. Just deduce the words or phrases represented by the fifteen letters A to O in the following fifteen sentences. One point only for each letter. (**Answers** on page 105.)

1 The A Guild secretary laughs: 'B. B. B.'

2 B is Djelibeybi's C-headed god of unexpected guests.

3 D will eat things that make a C sick. D will even eat C sick.

4 E and D are members of the same family.

5 The effective final score in the F Civil War was humans 0, E 1,000.

6 F was first seen ablaze at the beginning of G.

7 H is G.

8 After retirement, I worked in the H grass country.

9 Mr Pounder the J expert had a terminal encounter with the I of J.

10 Tuppence-worth of fresh J helped calm the K iconographer's craving.

11 One K of Uberwald, seemingly an old flame of a certain F notable, dabbled in local L politics.

12 The L and M races have an ancient, deadly rivalry.

13 The M roadie had been sat on by an N.

14 The device incorporating eight pottery N figures was based on a real-world O recorder.

15 A should *not* use the 128-foot O pipe.

Guild of Interpreters

Phrases in strange and mangled tongues, often the old language Latatian. Your mission, should you choose to accept it, is to translate them. (**Answers** on page 106.)

(**Answers** on page 106.)

1 Excretus Est Ex Altitudine (the fate of one coat of arms).
2 Homo Homini Lupus (an Uberwald motto).
3 'Can o' pee, anyone?'
4 Morituri Nolumus Mori.
5 Quod Subigo Farinam.
6 Doctorum Adamus cum Flabello Dulci.
7 Yennork (a werewolf term).
8 NULLUS ANXIETAS.
9 Non temetis messor.
10 Questa maladetta porta si blocca . . . (the 'Departure' aria).
11 Stercus, stercus, stercus . . .
12 Pencillium.

Unseen University – The Hoodwinkers

Yet another of Discworld's orders of wizardry, collecting questions about individual wizards who have lived and sometimes died during the 2,000-year history of Unseen University . . . (**Answers** on page 108.)

1 What trophy on Mustrum Ridcully's wall commemorated his youthful performance as a Rowing Brown for Unseen University?

2 What is the three-word phrase that has never been accepted as a valid part of any magical invocation since used by the late Funnit the Forgetful as a last-minute addition to his famously successful spell to destroy the entire tree he was sitting in?

3 We've all heard of the Hero With A Thousand Faces – but who represented this eternal champion's complement, the hero with a thousand retreating backs?

4 Who was promoted from Reader in Invisible Writings to Head of Inadvisably Applied Magic?

5 Who was appointed Egregious Professor of Cruel and Unusual Geography after the position was so unfortunately vacated in *The Last Continent*?

6 What faculty position was held by Dr A. A. Dinwiddie, D.M. (7th), D.Thau., B.Occ., M.Coll., B.F.?

7 Which wizard was unaccountably fond, at times of crisis, of shouting 'Yo!'?

8 Whose destiny had a solitary loophole that depended on doing the unthinkable (for a wizard) – throwing his staff away?

9 Who was briefed for a long journey with the simple instruction 'Be afraid. Be very afraid.'?

10 Which wizard invented the Rev Counter for Use in Ecclesiastical Areas?

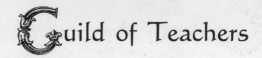uild of Teachers

Back to the schoolroom for a round of highly educational questions. You have all the time in the world to answer. Now turn over your papers and begin. (**Answers** on page 109.)

1 What's special about the striking of the Teachers' Guild clock?

2 What does Noxeuse's Divisibility Paradox prove about logs?

3 Of whom did former teacher Mr Saveloy immediately think when it was suggested he should be buried on top of the bodies of his enemies?

4 Who was the first and perhaps the stupidest pupil of Wen, founder of the History Monks?

5 What was the final examination question whose answer was 'wasp agaric, Achorion purple and Mustick'? (But not spime.)

6 Which man of letters was educated at the boarding school Hugglestones and left with a good report, mainly for being keen?

7 Which family's education featured surprise appearances of the double snake symbol of the Djelibeybian water cult and the All-Seeing Face of the Ionians?

8 How many silver 'pupil reward' stars in Susan's school class were the equivalent of one gold one?

9 Where might a student join The Ancient and Truly Original Brothers of the Silver Star?

10 Which educational establishment includes the girls-only BlackWidow House?

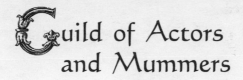uild of Actors and Mummers

Which Discworld characters were concealed behind each of the following disguises, impersonations and transformations? Allow yourself half a mark per answer where you've forgotten the character name(s) but can still identify the story or situation. (**Answers** on page 110.)

1 Beano the Clown.

2 Lord Vetinari, Patrician of Ankh-Morpork.

3 'Seven strange-looking old eunuchs, one of them in a wheeled contrivance.'

4 Jack Zweiblumen.

5 The armour of Queen Ynci the Short-Tempered, one of the founders of the kingdom of Lancre.

6 A humble but very, very efficient dairyman.

7 A group of obviously fake wizards wearing extremely obvious false beards.

8 A snowman with a carrot for a nose, holding a curved stick.

9 Molly, Queen of the Beggars, in her velvet cloak.

10 Gauze-clad exotic dancer Beti.

Guild of Merchants and Traders

Commerce is the lifeblood of a city, and sometimes Ankh-Morpork practically haemorrhages. What can you remember about Discworld's merchants, traders, vendors, hawkers, and shops? (**Answers** on page 112.)

1 According to scavenger Harry King, if the alchemists and even the farmers don't want it, there's nothing, *nothing*, however gross, that you can't sell to – whom?

2 What was stocked in the strange shop whose curious lever under the counter could move it to the other side of the road?

3 Which enterprising rubber merchant gave his name to Ankh-Morpork's favourite contraceptives?

4 What naughty Ankh-Morpork product, costing two dollars a pack in the Shades, was Colon's uncle disgusted to be asked AM$5 for in Klatch?

5 What is sold under a licence whose terms begin: 'This device is provided without warranty of any kind as to reliability, accuracy, existence or otherwise or fitness for any particular purpose . . .'

6 What is the one known product of Nonesuch Ecclesiastical Supplies, Ankh-Morpork?

7 Which (literal) seamstress runs a haberdashery shop and a lodging house, and is also a religious icon visited by pilgrims from afar?

8 Which doer of mighty deeds, slayer of dragons, and ravager of cities, once bought an apple?

9 What did the Seriph of Al Khali purchase from Ankh-Morpork at the cost of a cartload of figs each year?

10 What book about the city was published by this Guild?

Unseen University – The Order of Midnight

In a tradition inherited by Discworld's wizards from the 'Dying Earth' fantasy stories by Jack Vance, spells are generally known by their original creator's names. Match these names to the appropriate spells or magical effects below and spot the non-Discworld outsider: Atavaar, Bonza Charlie, Brother Hushmaster, Eringya, Fresnel, Gindle, Heisenberg, Phandaal, Stacklady, Sumpjumper. (**Answers** on page 113.)

1 Beaut Sieve.

2 Effortless Elevator.

3 Incendiary Surprise.

4 Mantle of Stealth.

5 Morphic Resonator.

6 Personal Gravitational Upset.

7 Potent Asp-Spray.

8 Surprising Bouquet.

9 Uncertainty Principle.

10 Wonderful Concentrator.

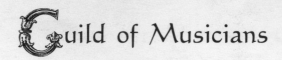

Guild of Musicians

'Do you know the answers to these?' 'No, but hum a few bars and I'll fake it ...' (**Answers** on page 114.)

1 What's the Discworld equivalent of 'Don't Cry for Me, Argentina'?

2 What Guild practice is liable to leave the trombonist feeling not very happy?

3 For what purposes, in rustic parts like Lancre, would one sing fifteen verses of 'Where Has All The Custard Gone?' under one's breath?

4 Why was it musically significant that Death borrowed the robe of the Dean of Unseen University (GIVE ME YOUR COAT) before riding out to the finale of *Soul Music*?

5 Which Discworld composer reminds us of our own world's George Frideric Handel (birth name Georg Friedrich Händel)?

6 Which folk tune popular among Discworld's Morris dancers is also, with one added letter, the name of an order of wizardry?

7 Which song is about – in Granny Weatherwax's words – a rodent that can't ever be persuaded to care about anything?

8 The UU students spent all night trying to teach the song 'Lydia the Tattooed Lady' to – whom?

9 What was the problem with Reg Shoe's rousing guitar performances of 'The Streets of Ankh-Morpork' and 'We Shall Overcome'?

10 Where could one hear a mighty B. S. Johnson organ playing 'Toccata for Young Women in Underwired Nightdresses'?

Thieves' Guild

A round of dodgy questions about shady characters . . . can you assist the Watch with their enquiries? (**Answers** on page 115.)

1 What's the official translation of the Guild's more or less Latin motto ACVTVS ID VERBERAT? Dictionaries may be consulted.

2 Whose tooth was used as bait to trap the Tooth Fairy?

3 Who committed the appalling social gaffe of arresting Urdo van Pew, President of the Guild of Thieves, Burglars and Allied Trades, for being a thief?

4 Which young Thieves' Guild member had a long fall and very nearly came to grief after discovering, atop the roof of the Bakers' Guild, that someone had loosened all the capping stones?

5 As Mrs Eulalie Butts thinks disapprovingly in *Soul Music*, the only guilds that think girls are worth educating are the Thieves and – which other?

6 What is particularly striking about the weathercock atop Guild headquarters in *Jingo*?

7 What did book thief Bengy 'Lightfoot' Boggis have in common with the legendary Fingers-Mazda who stole fire from the gods?

8 Whose aliases included The Park Lane Bully, Have You Seen This Man?, The Goose Gate Grabber, and The Nap Hill Lurker?

9 How do members of the affiliated Guild of Lags manage to turn a profit?

10 What is the undistinguished Klatchian desert city known in folklore as the place criminals always claimed to have been when accused of a crime?

Guild of Accountants

*Match your wits with the financial wizards of Ankh-Morpork, or at any rate match these Discworld regions with samples of their currencies as below ... derechmi, dongs, Krams, iotums (or would it be iota?), pennies, obols, rhinu, squids, talents, wols. (**Answers** on page 116.)*

1 Agatean Empire.
2 Djelibeybi.
3 Ephebe.
4 Hersheba.
5 Klatch.
6 Lancre.
7 Omnia.
8 Uberwald.
9 XXXX.
10 Zchloty.

Vitoller's Men

Here we visit the glamorous world of the stage, of actors and acting, of cardboard crowns and sagging tights ... (**Answers** on page 117.)

1 What is the name of Vitoller's theatre in Ankh-Morpork, echoing a historically famous one in London?

2 Which 1991 adaptation of a Discworld novel had to omit Death?

3 What part did Kring, the tediously verbose magic sword in *The Colour of Magic*, really want to play?

4 Which real-world assessment of a would-be performer is echoed by Silverfish's glum verdict on Victor Tugelbend in *Moving Pictures*: 'Can't sing. Can't dance. Can handle a sword a little'?

5 In which book did one of the play's Rude Mechanicals get into character with cries of 'Bum!', 'Drawers!' and 'Belly!'?

6 What remarkable ability did Shawn Ogg of Lancre share with the once famous French performer Le Pétomane?

7 Which Roundworld playwright (and novelist) is Death quoting in *Small Gods* when he uses the phrase HELL IS OTHER PEOPLE?

8 What other set of play-producing Men were rivals of Vitoller's?

9 What masked performance went roughly 'man gets girl, man loses girl to other man, man cuts couple in half, man falls on own sword . . .'?

10 The wyrd sisters in the cast list of *A Night of Kings* ('The Lancre Play') were Wethewacs, Ane Evil Witch; Hogg, Ane Likewise Evil Witch; and Magerat, Ane . . . what?

Embalmers' Guild

Grisly questions concerning sticky ends and post-mortem care. (**Answers** on page 118.)

1 Which Discworld novel introduced us to the traditional guild jest in which an embalmer – first suiting the action to the words – wittily remarks, 'Your name in lights.'

2 What dreadful thing did Williamson of the Clockmakers' Guild do to a clock that made his very *focused* colleague Jeremy murder him with a hammer?

3 A tour of Unseen University in *The Discworld Companion* includes a peep at bygone Archchancellor 'Trouter' Hopkins, whose will stipulated that his body should be embalmed in alcohol. So there he sits to this day, preserved in his niche – echoing the fate of which real-world academic?

4 Which legendary Guild leader, according to the harsh light of observation, returned from the grave as a set of ear-muffs and a pair of fleecy gloves?

5 The dying words of the sole survivor of the ship *Maria Pesto*, which was said to have travelled right under the Disc and returned on the far side, were: 'My God, it's full of . . .' What?

6 It was supposedly a case of mysterious spontaneous combustion: old Mr Hardy unfortunately lit a cigar and forgot he was bathing his feet in turpentine. As a cure for what?

7 What killed El-Ysa (not the name of a human character)?

8 What was the fatal blood condition suffered by the highwayman on the road to Lancre who unwisely delivered his challenge ('Your money or your life . . . Which part of this don't you understand?') to Death?

9 Who was reported, however improbably, to have choked to death on a concubine?

10 The Senior Wrangler's aunt had a fatal encounter: 'We couldn't get it off her. I *told* her that's not the way you're supposed to eat them, but . . .' What was it?

Country Landowners' Association

Besides owning large tracts of the Sto Plains, this Association is naturally interested in all Discworld's geography, politics and Mappes. Hubwards ho! (**Answers** on page 119.)

1 What is the Muntab question?

2 The desert land of the nomadic D'regs was disastrously partitioned by a dotted line marking the border between Klatch and . . . which country?

3 Why does one of the bridges of Ankh-Morpork remind you of some card game?

4 Which old country located Rimward of the kingdom of Djelibeybi sounds like a noise of conversational hesitation?

5 Of which continent is it said, 'The barman *everywhere* is from there?'

6 Which geographical feature of the Circle Sea appears only intermittently?

7 Which spooky country that no longer exists in our world is suggested by Discworld's Uberwald?

8 Which Discworld country inevitably contains the town of Pant-y-Girdl?

9 In which country can we find a scene similar to that described in Shelley's sonnet 'Ozymandias'?

10 From where does the Pointless Albatross carry messages to Ankh-Morpork?

11 What is the principal import of the region which Death calls A PLACE I CANNOT GO?

12 What is the principal export of Llamedos, which even has mines of the stuff?

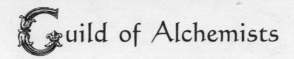

Guild of Alchemists

The Alchemists get a lot of bad publicity, alas, because so many of their innocent researches into natural science lead to loud bangs or, at best, hideous conflagrations. Hence these explosive and incendiary questions . . . (**Answers** on page 121.)

1 How would you detonate a 50-pound keg of Agatean Thunder Clay?

2 What excessively flammable substance was the basis of the short-lived Discworld 'clicks' industry?

3 What innocent purpose did Leonard of Quirm imagine for an otherwise useless metal that – when squeezed hard enough – goes bang 'With extreme alacrity'?

4 What name did the alchemist Silverfish give to the same (or a similar) useless-seeming, heavier-than-lead metal that offered hopes of 'a new, clear future . . .'?

5 In what Holy Wood production was a blazing stage set of Ankh-Morpork used to recreate a scene from the city's Civil War?

6 Where would you expect to find a Barking Dog?

7 What items of equipment for a well-known game, made by the Alchemists from nitro-cellulose and camphor, are unfortunately liable to take off in columns of flame, spin furiously on the spot, ricochet off the walls, and blow up?

8 What blaze started by a violently broken lamp produced a deadly shower of molten lead?

9 How was the inept wizard Rincewind able to blast a hole in the wall of the Forbidden City in Hunghung, merely by (or so it seemed) waving his hand?

10 In spite of all their talk of turning lead into gold, what is the one transformation which the Alchemists reliably achieve?

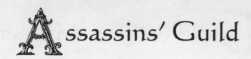

Assassins' Guild

As you answer these, don't look behind you . . . (**Answers** on page 123.)

1 According to *The Assassins' Guild Yearbook and Diary 2000*, the History tutor at the Guild college is Mr Linbury-Court. Which series of comic school novels does this suggest?

2 Which over-enthusiastic assassin worked out plans for the inhumation of such metaphysical beings as the Soul Cake Duck, the Sandman and even Death?

3 What object were the Assassins instructed by the Patrician himself to destroy, only for them to disobey?

4 Which street person, again according to the *Yearbook*, is the subject of an Assassin's Guild Open Commission to the value of one groat – one major difficulty being getting close enough?

5 Which high-ranking Assassin was personally killed by Corporal Carrot?

6 Which former Guild scholarship boy had, despite all his training, a fatal encounter with a very clever werewolf?

7 How did Guild member Miss Alice Band carry a 'Falchion' Compressed Air Device with Adjustable Timer Mechanism as a concealed weapon?

8 A particularly deadly plant, with no upper limit to its fatality, is the Sapu tree of Sumtri – reflecting which legendary killer on Roundworld?

9 Who is the best-known Klatchian to be an alumnus of the Assassins (Viper House)?

10 What was the smiling assassin Mr Teatime's first name?

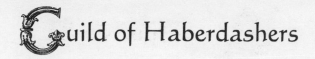

Guild of Haberdashers

Which accessories and minor articles of clothing had the following descriptions or properties? (**Answers** on page 124.)

1 Made by Mr Vernissage of Slice, it had willow reinforcement and eighteen internal pockets.

2 It was so big that when its owner sat clasping it on her lap, she had to reach up to hold the handles.

3 Very old and decorated with gold lace, pearls, bands of purest vermine, sparkling Ankhstones, tasteless sequins, and a circle of octarines.

4 They were made of red silk and ripped as the wearer's talons unfolded.

5 Fishing flies were stuck in it, and the tip unscrewed as a drinking horn for use with the bottle of Bentinck's Very Old Peculiar Brandy tucked inside.

6 A little one on a string to go with 'a pair of glasses onna stick, the whole thing' when poshly patronizing the Opera House.

7 It held, among other equipment, a dagger, a small glass phial and a number of metal rods with threaded ends.

8 Heavy, leather, reinforced with steel mesh, and worn by an orangutan.

9 The repository for three thousand, two hundred and seventy dollars and eighty-seven pence in cash.

10 Worn by the drivers of certain covered ox-carts entering Lancre, to cover embarrassing puncture marks.

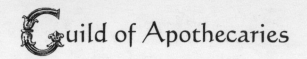

Guild of Apothecaries

Strange formulae and chemicals that you might buy (or might prefer not to) over the counter in a Discworld apothecary's shop. (**Answers** on page 125.)

1 Spirits of Nacle – used in conjunction with refined oil and chalk for faking which moderately rare art material?

2 The Alchemists' standard No. 1 Powder is required to load one of Leonard of Quirm's deadly inventions – what are its three ingredients?

3 Bloat, a favourite of the Assassins – producing what effect when administered?

4 Chloric ammonium mixed with radium – not sold to which customers in particular?

5 Mature scumble, pickled cucumbers, capers, mustard, mangoes, figs, grated wahooni, anchovy essence, asafetida, sulphur and saltpetre – adding up to what?

6 Meat, grain, a bag of mothballs and a pint of fish oil – the falconer's bait for what?

7 Molten sulphur on coke with phosphoric acid – requested by which member of the Watch?

8 Common sand and water – whose crazed architectural genius could possibly create an explosive mixture from this?

9 Chelonium, elephantigen and narrativium – believed by wizards to be necessary for what?

10 Assorted vegetables, beer, too much salt, beer, and prolonged heat – the recipe for what?

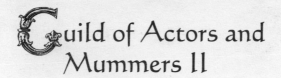uild of Actors and Mummers II

Once again, which Discworld characters were concealed behind each of the following disguises, impersonations and transformations? Once again, allow yourself half a mark per answer if you've forgotten the character name or names but can still identify the story or situation. (**Answers** on page 126.)

1 A large, blue, shoulder-mounted chicken that went 'cluck'.

2 A large hot-water bottle with a teddy-bear cover in red fur.

3 A poodle, more or less, of surpassing blow-dried pinkness, with a large glittery collar.

4 Although the Captain didn't like it, they wore plain clothes.

5 A pumpkin which in accordance with universal laws of humour still wore a hat.

6 A 'Mr Spuddy' potato-head outfit from the joke shop on Phedre Road.

7 The oldest, most unpleasant pixie in the universe, wearing a jolly little green hat with a bell on it.

8 Sister Jennifer, a nun from the order of The Little Flowers of Perpetual Annoyance.

9 A titled former courtesan in a stunning black silk dress (with jet beads and sequins) created for the Dowager Duchess of Quirm.

10 Not a human character, more an anthropomorphic personification: a spiky little green man who danced in dreams, crackling and gibbering.

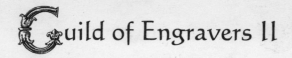

Guild of Engravers II

More signs, notices, placards, and graffiti – to be found in which book in each case? (**Answers** on page 127.)

1 GREASY FORANE HANDS OFF LESHP.

2 Slab: Jus' say 'AarrghaarrghpleeassennononoUGH.'

3 Old Faithful.

4 Gdy Mat. Look at the hinjis.

5 13 Midden Lane, Pseudopolis, Sto Plains, The Discworld, On top of Great A'tuin, The Univers, Space. nr. More Space.

6 GOE AWAY.

7 TO WORK IS TO LIVE.

8 THIS IS WHAT YOU DO.

9 Leave your common sense here.

10 Not to be used in any circumstances. This is IMPORTANT.

Unseen University –
Mrs Widgery's Lodgers

*Some questions that explore the secrets of the University itself,
ramifying as it does through eldritch dimensions of space, time,
architecture, and gluttony.* (**Answers** on page 128.)

1 What was the problem with room 5B that led even experienced wizards to cough before entering, in case of an alarming
encounter?

2 Which adolescent wizard practised Borrowing on the University building and learned for the first time what it was like to
have balconies?

3 What is Scholar's Entry?

4 What is so significant about the High Energy Magic department being in the University squash court?

5 What happened when the expedition into the Library to find
the Lost Reading Room – reduced after three weeks'
wandering to eating their own boots – found the remains of
the previous year's party?

6 What is unusual about the UU observatory used for viewing
. . . the *other* stars?

7 What post-mortem custom was introduced after the
embarrassing matter of the late wizard Prissal 'Merry Pranks-
ter' Teatar (who used to put green paint on his face, push the
lid off the coffin and shout 'Surprise, surprise')?

8 What feature of the University safe made it so improbable that
the Bursar kept locking himself and the key inside?

9 Why has the circular vestibule between UU's Great Hall and its main door been known since antiquity as Archchancellor Bowell's Remembrance?

10 Which University building is about twenty feet high from the bottom, but half a mile high at the top?

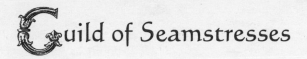

Guild of Seamstresses

It is well known that 'seamstresses' is the polite Ankh-Morpork euphemism for ladies of negotiable affection, and that 'house of ill repute' is an inappropriate phrase since Mrs Rosemary Palm's place actually has a jolly good repute. (**Answers** on page 129.)

1 A nice easy one to open: who is President of the Guild of Seamstresses?

2 Who, after rescuing young seamstress Reet from robbers, became perhaps the first man to stay at Mrs Palm's under the impression that it was a boarding house?

3 This Guild represents not the oldest but the second oldest profession on Discworld. What's the oldest?

4 Who claimed to have joined the City Watch as a last resort, since it was either that or become a seamstress?

5 Which innocent from Lancre tried to get a job at the Guild and took along some examples of stitching?

6 Mrs Palm's committee of very experienced ladies laid down the *unwritten rules* of the business – enforced by which painful pair?

7 What Klatchian book of exotic sexual pleasures echoes a famous Roundworld text with 'Garden' in the title?

8 What was the unintended (thanks to a spelling error) subject matter of the spicy manual ordered by royalty for intimate purposes but in the event given to Shawn Ogg?

9 Who hoped to encounter 'mysterious ancient races of Amazonian princesses who subject all male prisoners to strange and exhausting progenitative rites'?

10 Which Ankh-Morpork notable shares a forename with the author of our Roundworld's *Studies in the Psychology of Sex*?

The Librarians of Time and Space II

A round of bookish questions about books . . . (**Answers** on page 130.)

1 Which novel's working title was *Words in the Head*?

2 Which novel is dedicated to the person who first asked the question?

3 The 1997 *Encyclopedia of Fantasy*'s superb entry on Pratchett mentions how 'an aged schoolmaster who expected a dull afterworld shifts Stories to gatecrash Valhalla'. Who?

4 Which Discworld book had three authors, all named on the front cover?

5 Which Discworld-related book had three editors, all named on the front cover?

6 Which of the above three editors also wrote the Pocket Essentials guide to Terry Pratchett, published 2001?

7 What is the 'foreign' (far side of the Ramtop Mountains) equivalent of *Twurp's Peerage*, the standard reference on the aristocracy of Ankh-Morpork and surrounding lands?

8 Which Ankh-Morpork Guild, whose shield is bisected by a band, is important enough to have its own entry in *The Discworld Companion* (both 1994 and 1997 editions) but not in that book's 'Guilds' entry?

9 Which Discworld story is, very unusually, divided into 23 distinct chapters?

10 Where were Josh Kirby's first, unused cover paintings for *Moving Pictures* and *Jingo* eventually published?

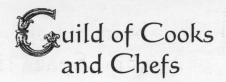

Guild of Cooks and Chefs

From the greasy inferno of Harga's House of Ribs to posh restaurants and the Patrician's Palace, the cooks are everywhere. . . . (**Answers** on page 131.)

1 Whose Hogswatch feast's many courses included this one: 'A medley of lobster, crab, King crab, prawn, shrimp, oyster, clam, Giant mussel, Green-lipped mussel, Thin-lipped mussel and Fighting Tiger limpet.' (Plus drinks.)

2 What does the traditional Ankh-Morpork dish fikkun haddock remind you of?

3 What was Merckle and Stingbat's Very Famous culinary product?

4 The Curious Squid, much prized by gourmets, is reckoned to have the foulest taste of any creature in the world. How do skilled chefs rise to this challenge?

5 What strange pink stuff in Uberwald's sausages was viewed with alarm and suspicion by a visitor from Ankh-Morpork?

6 Whose recipe for Chocolate Delight with Special Secret Sauce had (in most cases) disastrously inflaming effects?

7 What breadlike creation of great importance to dwarf politics was duplicated in Ankh-Morpork?

8 Who hoped to create instant fish and chips but so far had achieved only swimming potatoes?

9 Where could they make a handful of mud, a few dead leaves and some unpronounceable herbs into something that made gourmets shed tears of gratitude?

10 Who was able to reach into any hole in the desert and pull out dessert, for example a plate of chocolate-covered sponge cakes with dried coconut flakes on them?

11 What surprising dish is the approximate dwarf equivalent of the Cornish delicacy star-gazey pie?

12 'Alligator sandwich. And make it snappy!' Which cook actually served one up before the last word of this jokey order was completed?

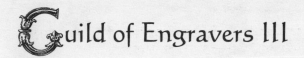

Guild of Engravers lll

The Engravers had a monopoly on book production for the first 24 Discworld novels, and these questions deal with books found or sought after on Discworld. (**Answers** on page 133.)

1 Who had a bad attack of management theory after getting hold of *How to Dynamically Manage People in a Caring Empowering Way in Quite a Short Time Dynamically*?

2 Which dread volume was unwisely used by the Elucidated Brethren of the Ebon Night?

3 In which storybook would one find the tale of the Glass Clock of Bad Schüschein?

4 Which Discworld religion has *Malleus Maleficarum* as one of its holy works?

5 What was the title of the revolutionary tract that convulsed the Agatean Empire?

6 What kind of press was associated with a collector's album and Walnut's *Inoffensive Reptiles of the Sto Plains*?

7 When marooned on an unpopulated island, the wizards' first escape plan was to search for a copy of what?

8 Where do we learn of W. H. J. Whittleby's *Guide to Impossible Buildings*, which discusses the homes (and their architecture) of the Hogfather, the Tooth Fairy, Time, and Death?

9 Where on Discworld can one find the recipe for Bananana Soup Surprise?

10 What was our world's equivalent of the ancient military treatise that some said was by One Tzu Sung and others by Three Sun Sung?

Minor Guilds and Societies II

Further probes into the doings of organizations which never somehow rise to the fame of Assassins, Thieves or Wizards.... (**Answers** on page 134.)

1 What did the Guilds of Towncriers and Engravers agree in deploring?

2 With which unsavoury profession were the Plumbers joined in a single guild?

3 Which Guild had gross earnings of AM$7,999,011, paid no taxes, but applied for a rebate of AM$200,000?

4 Of which Guild were Wienrich and Boettcher the most droolingly well-regarded representatives in Ankh-Morpork?

5 The flat-roofed constructions of Thaumatological Park had won several awards from which Guild?

6 What, according to *The Discworld Companion*, is the Guild with the smallest membership of all, established under ancient rules that were changed very soon after the founder invoked them?

7 To which Guild would you expect the Amazing Bonko and Doris to belong?

8 Which Guild's All-Comers Hiccuping Contest provided an alchemical simile in *Feet of Clay*?

9 What was the guild of Mr Potts, whose coat of arms carried a rose, a flame and a water-pot (the last punning on his name)?

10 In which book are we introduced to the Guild of Victims, founded by Mr Echinoid Blacksly, who charges money to be mugged, burgled or robbed in place of his clients?

Unseen University: The Venerable Council of Seers

*In the fast-paced modern world of wizarding, it's essential to know what acronyms and initials stand for. Here's a selection to test your memory, with just a hint of context. (**Answers** on page 135.)*

1 Accommodation: YMPA.
2 Cartography: MMBU.
3 Cryptography: ENIGMA.
4 Fat-mining: BCBs.
5 Hagiology: STU.
6 Hardware: GBL, as in 'Initialize the GBL.'
7 Inexorability: WYGIWYGAINGW (a saying of Ridcully's).
8 Monkey business: SAS.
9 Resurgency: sought in the big ledger under F, eventually located under P.
10 Versatility: BSJ.

Campaign for Equal Heights

There will be absolutely no mentions in this section of lawn ornaments. And no looking down on our fellow citizens either. Thank you. (**Answers** on page 137.)

1 What, according to William de Worde in *The Truth*, is the humorous outcome of calling a dwarf 'short stuff'?

2 Which ruby-coloured articles of which witch's clothing did a band of dwarfs (helplessly caught by the power of Story) ask for after a house fell out of the sky?

3 What is the biggest dwarf city outside Uberwald?

4 Who did Mrs Cosmopilite (of 3 Quirm Street, Ankh-Morpork) believe peered in at her as she undressed each night?

5 Which dwarf highwayman climbed a small stepladder in order to kick the coachman in the middle of the road?

6 Why did the Committee for Equal Heights object to Stronginthearm's Iron Founders, Beaters and General Forging (Five and Seven Yard, Ankh-Morpork)?

7 What other literary dwarf suggested the name of Gimlet, who runs that delicatessen in Cable Street?

8 Where does the dwarf Modo tend the compost heaps?

9 Which dwarf was partnered with a traditional enemy of his race as a crime-fighting duo?

10 At which outdoor, rustic event did the dwarf Zakzak Stronginthearm do a roaring trade in 'Lucky Horseshoes $2 Each'?

11 In a dwarf bar, it's suicide to ask for . . . what?

12 Which very small entrepreneur had a nasty encounter with the enforcers of the Ratcatchers' Guild?

The Librarians of Time and Space III

Another round of questions about Discworld's subtle L-Space links with the familiar Roundworld where you're reading this. (**Answers** on page 138.)

1 'When a man is tired of Ankh-Morpork he is tired of ankle-dccp slurry,' said Discworld's philosopher Catroaster – echoing which Roundworld celebrity's comment about London?

2 Unseen University Library requires users to promise 'not to bring into the Library or kindle therein any fire or flame' – echoing which Roundworld library declaration?

3 Which monastic person is strangely reminiscent of his soundalike in a world-famous movie series co-produced by Harry Saltzman and Albert Broccoli?

4 Which Discworld artist seems at one point to have taken inspiration from the immortal *Peanuts* by Charles Schulz?

5 Who wrote the verses echoed by this line from *Hogfather*: 'It was the night before Hogswatch. All through the house . . .'

6 Who is the Roundworld historical equivalent of the vampiric Aunt Carmilla, who in *Carpe Jugulum* is said to have bathed in the blood of up to 200 virgins at a time?

7 Same character, different connection: who wrote the classic Roundworld story about a vampire named Carmilla?

8 Rincewind in *The Last Hero* is confounded by the Patrician's explanation that being either sane or insane qualifies him for a dangerous mission. 'I think there's a catch there,' he says, and is answered: 'The best kind there is.' What's the allusion?

9 Who is Carrot quoting in *Jingo* when he says 'My strength is as the strength of ten because my heart is pure'?

10 The Discworld equivalent of fell walker Alfred Wainright –
    who notoriously took his wire cutters to fences closing rights
    of way – is the even more gung-ho Eric Wheelbrace: 'Saw
    through any fences you see . . .' Where can he be found?

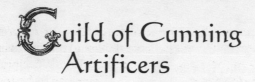

Guild of Cunning Artificers

The Street of Cunning Artificers has long been a feature of Ankh-Morpork, and there is an associated Guild of Cunning Artificers. Here, therefore, are questions about cunning artifices. (**Answers** on page 140.)

1 Which multipurpose gadget for the use of armed forces was to include nose-hair tweezers, a folding saw, and an Adjustable Device for Winning Ontological Arguments?

2 What is the proverbial name for the History Monks' rotating cylinders that manipulate time in *Thief of Time*?

3 What three-ton, water-driven device enabled the Watch to make three arrests after a sneaky change to its inner workings?

4 What was the actual, practical use of the B. S. Johnson gadget whose brass plate said 'Improved Manicure Device'?

5 Which hellish pocket device repeatedly went 'Bingely-bingely beep!'?

6 Which very loud, pressurized machine, originally intended as a scale model of a device for reaching the moon and other celestial bodies, was adapted for another purpose by the thirsty Leonard of Quirm and began its operations by going *Blup*?

7 Which intricate device consisted mainly of two discs, one carrying tiny squares of carpet and the other having many arms bearing very small slices of buttered toast?

8 What looked like a long-handled hammer or strangely made telescope, and was strictly forbidden within Ankh-Morpork by both the Watch and the Assassins' Guild?

9 Who designed a flying machine whose control levers had such labels as 'Troba' and 'Sekarb'?

10 What mechanical creation of young 'Rubber' Houser became so popular that pupils kept breaking the rules in order to use it?

11 One of Leonard of Quirm's most practical inventions, since it operated '*submersed* in a *marine* environment', was named by him . . . what?

12 What, on Discworld, was named after its inventor Sir Charles?

Guild of Shoemakers and Leatherworkers

Simply identify a selection of items associated with this Guild's activities . . . (**Answers** on page 142.)

1 Very short, home-made planks with a loop of twine for the toe, impossible to run in but easy to leave behind.

2 Old Shaker Wistley of Creel Springs used to collect these, and 'If he saw you going past in a new pair he had to go and have a lie down.'

3 They had pink pompoms on them, and were a dreadful embarrassment for a captain of the Watch to be seen wearing.

4 Magical prototypes which imposed unfortunate groinal strains; the test subject had to wear a special device for several months, and ate standing up.

5 Always carried needle and thread for stitching bits back on.

6 Mr Seldom Bucket complained that they cost a ruinous seven dollar a pair and lasted hardly any time at all.

7 Mirror-surfaced with dozens of facets that caught the light.

8 Affordable, sort of okay for a season or two, and then leaked like hell when the cardboard gave out.

9 Spontaneously changed to blue suede under the insidious influence of Music With Rocks In.

10 They had complicated iron fixtures, and toecaps like battering rams.

11 Where to buy rubberwork, and feathers, and whips, and little jiggly things.

12 When the gods marvel at a planet whose people displayed only mild interest at the sight of huge continent-wrecking slabs of ice slapping into another world practically next door, what event do they have in mind?

Priests', Sacerdotes' and Occult Intermediaries' Guild

It's a tough life being a man of God in a world where the gods are so very numerous, provable and stroppy. (**Answers** on page 144.)

1 What is the name and rank of Archchancellor Mustrum Ridcully's more religious brother?

2 Of which incarnated god was it frequently said, generally by his own supposed worshippers, 'There's good eating on one of those'?

3 Which god was troubled by seeing indigo-coloured giraffes 'which are sort of stretched and keep flashing on and off'?

4 Which earnest priest of the Omnian god Om nevertheless burned his prized *Book of Om*?

5 What unusual type of atheist successfully defies the lightning of the gods, without special protection?

6 What four cruel and insupportable food restrictions are placed upon followers of the god Nuggan?

7 Which god, echoing a remark by scientist J. B. S. Haldane, had an inordinate fondness for beetles?

8 Which supernatural entity, when choking, was subjected to the Heimlich manoeuvre?

9 Complete this ecclesiastical organization with a stony phrase: 'Council of Churches, Temples, Sacred Groves and . . .'

10 The God of things left on the doorstep or half-digested under the bed has a non-human head – what kind?

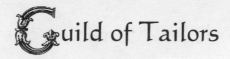uild of Tailors

Further questions about clothing and the like . . . (**Answers** on page 146.)

1 Who appeared in a red suit with a red cloak, set off by various accessories all in red?

2 Who designed himself a black armless vest with innumerable useful pockets, a red silk lining, and tails?

3 Who was concealed by the piano with suspiciously many legs, from which came the enigmatic words, 'We're on a mission from Glod'?

4 Whose rather short body, clad in elegant clothes with grubby lace at the sleeves and a wide hat, gave the impression of a well-dressed mushroom with a feather on it?

5 Who got over-excited in a leather robe with BORN TO RUNE outlined in studs on the back?

6 Why did Miss Flitworth, disappointed on her wedding day, consider that life expected her to moon around the place for years in a wedding dress and go completely doolally?

7 Which group wore waist-length robes, shorts, long grey socks and big leather sandals?

8 Nothing could be finer than these formal outfits, short of 'inflating a Bird of Paradise, possibly by using an elastic band and some kind of gas'.

9 Which small person's too-long opera cloak trailed on the floor 'to give the overall impression of a superhero who had spent too much time around the Kryptonite'?

10 Whose waterproof mackintosh was made (with a bit of scissor-work) from a Big Boy?

Ankh-Morpork City Watch II

Once again, would-be Watchmen are invited to spot the suspicious character or item that's the odd one out in these brief lists. (**Answers** on page 148.)

1 Adulteratedly: milk, chocolate, sugar, suet, hooves, lips, miscellaneous squeezings, rat droppings, plaster, flies, tallow, bits of tree, hair, lint, spiders, powdered cocoa husks.

2 Belatedly: Cuddy, Corporal Curry, Herbert 'Leggy' Gaskin, Sgt Maroon, Reg Shoe.

3 Bibliographically: *Bows and Ammo, Warrior of Fortune, The Use of Pliers in Warfare, Practical Siege Weapons.*

4 Gastronomically: walago, noggi, sclot, swineflesh, noggo.

5 Hallucinogenically: Clang, Slip, Chop, Rhino, Xeno, Skunk, Triplin.

6 Heroically: Bruce the Hoon, Crowdie the Strong, The Immortal Jenkins, Organdy Sloggo, Thog the Butcher, Voltan the Indestructible.

7 Logically: AND, OR, MAYBE, REDO, PERHAPS, SUPPOSE, WHY.

8 Nominally: Big, Fat, Mad, Medium, Wee, Lanky.

9 Optically: Quoth the Raven, Norris the maniac of Quirm, Samuel Vimes, Susan's school class at dessert.

10 Witchily: books of spells, last will and testament, small private universe, cures for all ills, deeds of lost lands.

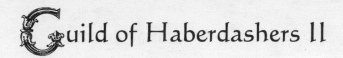

Guild of Haberdashers II

More strange accessories and fripperies which may or may not have been worn by Discworld characters . . . (**Answers** on page 150.)

1 Items of ducal regalia which Vimes found even more appalling than the puffed sleeves and red tights of his dress uniform as Commander of the Watch.

2 A crowning glory that seemed unusually, perhaps even unnaturally . . . sparkly. Fishnet tights tend to lurk in the vicinity.

3 In the amusingly named town of Bonk, which half of a better known city's name sounds exactly like their word for an item of ladies' underwear?

4 Like an ostrich head coloured violent yellow with a ruff of red and purple feathers and drunkenly jiggling eyes.

5 What, in modern times, are naughty children apt to receive as Hogswatch presents instead of the traditional bag of bloody bones?

6 It was huge and black and had things on it, like bird wings and wax cherries and hatpins; its owner travelled underneath it as the basket travels under a balloon.

7 Who is invariably baffled when asked why he has one on his head?

8 Extraordinarily thick ones were advisable for those crossing the thorny moorland to the gnarly country.

9 What had dangling bottles attached until the realization that it would be better with just corks?

10 Which of Samuel Vimes's possessions did Lady Sybil warn that she would utilize for hosiery accessories?

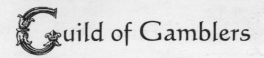

Guild of Gamblers

What's the odds? And in which Discworld books were the same odds stated for the following very unlikely occurrences? But it might just work . . . (**Answers** on page 152.)

1 Getting back the staff she'd thrown in the now rapidly flooding river.

2 '. . . the chances of a man with soot on his face, his tongue sticking out, standing on one leg and singing *The Hedgehog Song* ever hitting a dragon's voonerables . . .'

3 REALITY WOULD NEED TO BE WEAKENED IN CERTAIN ELDRITCH WAYS.

4 '. . . that blade will work, will it?'

5 'You think she's going to be sent to the ball in a *pumpkin*, eh?'

6 'There was only one way to get to the Citadel now.'

7 'I don't understand all this continuinuinuum stuff, but from what young Stibbons says it means that everything has to happen somewhere, d'y'see, so that means it could happen here.'

8 '. . . the invisible horsemen known as Misinformation, Rumour and Gossip saddled up . . .'

9 'Just hit it below the waterline so they can't cut the rope.'

10 Working out whether there's enough air outside the ship for Leonard to steer it . . .

The Librarians of Time and Space IV

Yet more on Discworld's morphological connections with our own Roundworld . . . (**Answers** on page 153.)

1 Where does Samuel Vimes, on the run, find himself in Chekhov country?

2 Why should the Ankh-Morpork Historical Re-creation Society in *Feet of Clay* be commonly known as the Peeled Nuts?

3 What is the Roundworld equivalent of Leonard of Quirm's 'Make Words With Letters That Have Been All Mixed Up Game'?

4 Lord Vetinari, considering flying machines in *The Last Hero*, recollects an old story about 'a ship that was pulled by swans and flew all the way to . . .' He doesn't complete the sentence, but what was the destination of the space mission powered by swans (or wild geese) and described in a real-world book published in the 17th century?

5 The question 'what use is a new-born child' is briefly considered in *The Science of Discworld*; which real-world inventor said approximately this?

6 Which long-ago media favourite featured the wily Arab whose catchphrase – like Ahmed's when hamming it up in *Jingo* – was 'I go, I come back'?

7 Which bygone British children's TV show was hinted at when the already overburdened hero of *Pyramids* was required to hold the Cabbage of Vegetative Increase?

8 Whose ancestor was Ankh-Morpork's Oliver Cromwell?

9 Which Roundworld children's fantasy novel from the 1860s relates to Sgt Colon's rooted dislike of the sea?

10 How does a 1926 thriller title by Edgar Wallace link to the Discworld puzzle whose key is Woddeley's Occult Sequence?

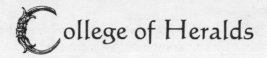

College of Heralds

Heralds are the people who know all about names, families, relationships and descent . . . (**Answers** on page 155.)

1 Which Patrician of Ankh-Morpork was the immediate predecessor of the current Lord Vetinari?

2 Which high-level wizard was annoyed at being successively called Mappin Winterley, Owen Houseworthy, William, Gertrude, and Charlie Grinder?

3 Whose opening remarks included the phrase 'you can call me Mister Boring if you like', persuading would-be summoners of demons that he was a demon called Boring?

4 Who brightly said to the wizards, 'We don't want to be Mr Grumpy, do we?'

5 Which creature's various names included Call-me-Mr-Thumpy-and-die?

6 Whose family motto was *Le Mot Juste*?

7 Who was shamefully nicknamed Trunkie?

8 What is the appropriate name of the Discworld God of Wine, corresponding to Roundworld's legendary Bacchus?

9 Which family's coat of arms punningly suggests the surname *via* a bunch of grapes?

10 Why does one suspect that Ankh-Morpork's noble old family the Selachii had its roots in financial, not to say fishy, affairs?

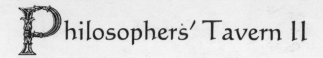

Philosophers' Tavern II

Both here and on Discworld, low-budget philosophy can take the form of well-worn proverbs and catchphrases – though sometimes, in the Pratchett universe, they mutate. Fill in the missing words indicated by XXXX . . . (**Answers** on page 156.)

1 'The Buck XXXX Here.'

2 Carrot: 'Is the XXXX XXXX an Offlian?'

3 Igor to Vimes: 'The marthter does not drink . . . XXXX?'

4 Nanny Ogg: 'The leopard does not change his XXXX, my girl!'

5 Susan: 'Does a bear XXXX in the woods?'

6 Carrot: 'Does a dragon XXXX in the woods?'

7 Carrot: 'Does a camel XXXX in the XXXX, sir?'

8 Bilious: 'The XXXX is on the other boot now, eh?'

9 Dhblah: 'A nod's as good as a poke with a sharp stick to a XXXX XXXX.'

10 Nanny Ogg: 'There's many a slip twixt XXXX and XXXX.'

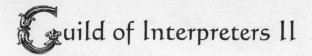

Guild of Interpreters II

Here are translation questions that go in the other direction, working back from common-speech definitions to the antique, foreign or jargon originals. (**Answers** on page 157.)

1 What is the technical term for someone who like Archchancellor Ridcully regards meals as no more than a foundation for salt, pepper, mustard, pickles, ketchup and sauce?

2 What is the word for a secret copying process in which 'each one must be the same as the one before'?

3 What's the Quirmian for the duties of nobs – giving to charity, being kind to the poor, and so on?

4 What's the Klatchian for 'mouth-scalding gristle for macho foreign idiots'?

5 What grandiose theatrical term was translated by Nanny Ogg as 'blood all over the stage'?

6 Which word of the old language, linked to iconography, very understandably means 'To prance around like a pillock ordering everyone about as if you owned the place'?

7 Who was mistakenly translated as a small red breakfast roll?

8 What word can mean (in Howandaland) 'Highly enjoyable', 'Your wife is a big hippo', and indeed 'Hello, Thinks Mr Purple Cat'?

9 What is the engraved Watch-house motto officially translated as 'To Protect and to Serve'?

10 What word was coined to describe Nobby Nobbs's unique social quality of being so dreadful he fascinates people?

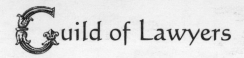

Guild of Lawyers

A round of questions about rules and regulations, although sometimes they're more just . . . guidelines. (**Answers** on page 158.)

1 In which high place is 'No Smiting' one of the local rules?

2 What is the important repeated message of Lu Tze's Rule Nineteen?

3 Which card game's rules did Death confess (in *Maskerade*) that he'd never been able to understand?

4 What subtle art's rules were: 'you didn't hurt, you just rode inside their heads, you didn't *involve* the subject in any way'?

5 Which Ankh-Morpork ethnic minority had an inbuilt resistance even to the invisible rules that most people obey unthinkingly, like 'Do not attempt to eat this giraffe'?

6 To what does Ponder Stibbons's Rule Three – 'You get balls' – apply?

7 What was the rule that forced the Tooth Fairy to use the pliers?

8 Where is it a rule that no one can even go to the privy without written permission?

9 According to Rincewind, one of the most basic rules for survival on any planet is never to upset anyone wearing black what?

10 Which far-flung organization's Rule Three is, 'Do not interfere with the nature of causality'?

Guild of Actors and Mummers III

A theatrical theme, or item of stage property, links all these . . . answer the question or identify the item in each case. (**Answers** on page 159.)

1 Who was forced to wear a gold one called the Face of the Sun?

2 Who was delighted to wear a ginger one to the ball?

3 Who wore one as smooth and white as the skull of an angel?

4 How Ridcully imitated Willie the Vampire in an unsuccessful attempt to buck up the Bursar and take him out of himself.

5 A small girl told Bill Door that she had one for Soul Cake Night, adding 'You get given sweets.'

6 This was Lu Tze's unexpected, but unoriginal, Fifth Surprise.

7 As the villain said, without it 'he's an idiot who can hardly tie his shoelaces!!!!' Who?

8 Where was the guest who said I'M HERE INCOGNITO congratulated by a nervous butler for having a damn good one?

9 It was suggested that the Patrician's lookalike might be issued with one and locked up – like the title character of which Alexandre Dumas novel?

10 Which inspired playwright found a place for a villain who used one to conceal his disfigurement?

Guild of Merchants and Traders II

This round of questions is dedicated to the Discworld's greengrocers or, as they would probably prefer to write it, the Discworlds greengrocer's. (**Answers** on page 161.)

1 What fruit, according to Ponder Stibbons's understanding of cladistics, is botanically a type of fish?

2 Which plant's root, for reasons unknown to cattle, features in their visions of the happy afterlife?

3 What is the principal food crop of Scrote and the surrounding Sto Plains, even lending its name to a tavern?

4 What kind of fruit did Percy Hopcroft ingratiatingly name after Nanny Ogg?

5 Who was apparently reincarnated as a not at all humorous vegetable?

6 What fruit is invoked to persuade legendary pigs to fly?

7 What Igor-created fruiting plant growled and rocked from side to side in its box?

8 What by-product of the Royal College of Heralds caused rhubarb to grow twenty feet tall and then spontaneously catch fire?

9 Insert vegetables to complete Nellie Stamp's music-hall song title from *Maskerade*: 'She Sits Among the XXXX and XXXX'.

10 What vegetable is twenty feet long, covered in spikes the colour of earwax, and smells so awful that it's banned in many cities?

Cable Street Particulars

Here are questions about the inner workings of the Ankh-Morpork Watch itself. You have the right to remain silent . . . (**Answers** on page 162.)

1 What tragic event that kept Corporal Nobbs away from his Watch duties allegedly happened on seven separate occasions one year?

2 What was the greatest excess of the somewhat over-enthusiastic Watch traffic control and wheel-clamping unit?

3 Name any of the religious newsletters or magazines pressed on colleagues by the Constable nicknamed Washpot.

4 In what unusual currency was Constable Downspout paid?

5 Whose civilian disguise when investigating at the Opera House was slightly spoilt by keeping his Watch helmet on?

6 Who joined the Watch after an embarrassingly misguided application to the Guild of Seamstresses?

7 Which late recruit to the Watch has the same name and species as a minor character in the second Discworld novel?

8 Who was of the same religious persuasion as his friend Smite-The-Unbeliever-With-Cunning-Arguments?

9 In which dark adventure did ex-Watchman Lewton star as Discworld's first private eye?

10 What made Carrot connect Watch recruitment of ethnic minorities with the dwarf Grabpot Thundergust's cosmetics factory?

Guild of Fools and Joculators II

When is a door not a door? When, of course, it's a cylindrical glass receptacle suitable for holding jam. Brace yourself for metacosmic analysis of punes, or plays on words. . . . (**Answers** on page 163.)

1 What was considered as a retirement present 'from, your Old Freinds in the Watch'?

2 Ridcully: 'What kind of bird stops flyin' around for a quick smoke?'

3 Sgt Colon to Nobby: 'I bet you was *born* hoping that one day someone'd say "That's a harp" so you could say . . .' What?

4 Which martial art twists time so that a prepared opponent can be surprised from behind?

5 Sgt Colon to Vimes: 'You always been dead against . . .' What?

6 Death to the unfortunate dwarf Bjorn Hammerhock: SINCE YOU BELIEVE IN REINCARNATION . . . what?

7 William de Worde to Dibbler on being told that times are hard in the hot sausage trade: 'Can't make both . . .' What?

8 Ridcully welcomes foreign royalty to the Convivium: 'we'll be ready in a brace of . . .' What?

9 Legendary musician Brother Charnel had his instrument made from stolen gold and therefore gained jazz immortality as a . . . what?

10 A giant pumpkin in the form of a ship has room for all the wizards: 'Even if it is a bit of a . . .' What?

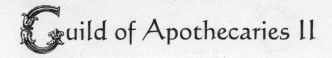

Guild of Apothecaries II

Further strange formulae and perverse prescriptions . . .
(**Answers** on page 164.)

1 Bath salts, bath soap, bubble bath, herbal bath lumps, tons of bath stuff – tactful festive gifts for whom?

2 A glass of water, a spoonful of acid, two lengths of wire and a ping-pong ball – Leonard's recipe for accidentally blowing up what?

3 'Rare herbs and suchlike . . . Including suckrose and akwa.' – prescribed by whom as placebo medicine for Jarge Weaver's bad back?

4 Oil of aniseed, oil of rampion and oil of scallatine – used to distract which pursuing member of the Watch?

5 Essence of spikkle mixed with oatmeal – good for dealing with what kind of infestation?

6 Orange juice, crusty bread, and drinking your own urine . . . the key to what, according to alchemists?

7 L-O-T-S-O-F-D-R-Y-D-F-R-O-R-G-P-$\frac{1}{4}$-I-L-L-S – medicine for whom?

8 *Aqua Quirmis* – the equivalent of which dangerous Round-world acid?

9 Copper rods, zinc rods, and a lemon – Leonard's ingredients for what?

10 Three small bits of wood and 4cc of mouse blood, or even two bits of wood and a fresh egg – who ya gonna call?

Guild of Engravers and Printers

*There comes a time in the Discworld sequence when a Guild name has to change ... and there's considerable upheaval when the Engravers' Guild reaches the watershed of history. It's also the occasion for a whole lot of Roundworld allusions which you are pressed to clarify. (**Answers** on page 165.)*

1 Goodmountain the dwarf.

2 William de Worde the letter-writer ('Things Written Down').

3 Boddonny the dwarf.

4 The motto 'The Truth Shall Make Ye Free.' (Or 'Fret'. Or 'Fred'.)

5 Caslong the dwarf.

6 The discovery in the Watch House that rats have been nibbling at the pneumatic speaking tubes. (A Victorian railway allusion.)

7 Gowdie the dwarf.

8 King of the Golden River.

9 Lord de Worde's 'Publish and be damned.'

10 The Patrician's observation: 'Bribed? ... My dear sir, seeing what you're capable of for nothing, I'd hesitate to press even a penny in your hand.'

Campaign for Dead Rights

They'll be back. In fact, they never really went. (**Answers** on page 167.)

1   What's the bar where the undead of Ankh-Morpork drink?

2   What vampiric fruit are mentioned early in *Carpe Jugulum*?

3   Which ethnic minority did Mrs Drull belong to, and why should one never accept her meat patties?

4   In the law firm Morecambe, Slant and Honeyplace, what were Morecambe and Honeyplace?

5   Which ethnic minority is best subdued using a small piece of blue fluffy blanket?

6   Who was buried, somewhat reluctantly, at the junction of Ankh-Morpork's two busiest streets?

7   Whose return from the grave echoed the Frank Sinatra album title *Old Blue Eyes is Back*?

8   Who, in the Klatchian campaign, developed a particularly intimidating method of unarmed combat?

9   What magical commercial operation was headed by the first of all the bogeymen?

10 Of which ethnic minority was the chap whose series of unfortunate accidents included one in a pencil factory?

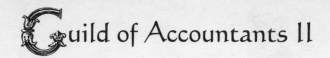

Guild of Accountants II

From Ankh-Morpork's experts on figures, a simple test on notable numbers featured in the Discworld saga. Note the careful omission of seven plus one *or, indeed,* twice four. (**Answers** on page 169.)

1 Average in years, about 11; in evil, about 163.

2 Mr Boggis of the Thieves' Guild was prepared to exchange his wife for 15 . . . what?

3 It was Volume 29c, Part Three, of a very extensive guide to dangerous animals of . . . where?

4 58 of these would be sold by the diminutive hunter for two a penny: the skins of what?

5 71.

6 Badge number 177.

7 There were 512 on the Temple door.

8 It fired a small stone cherub 1,000 feet into the air.

9 70,000 of them weigh almost a third of a ton.

10 ONE MILLION, EIGHT HUNDRED THOUSAND, SEVEN HUNDRED AND SIX . . . glasses of what?

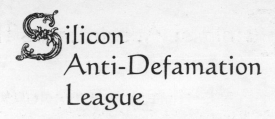

Silicon Anti-Defamation League

A round of questions about those interesting folk with names like Rock, Cliff, Crag and Bauxite. (**Answers** on page 170.)

1 What dread monster was impersonated by Morry (Morraine) with the aid of wings and some green paint?

2 Who found soaring intellectual inspiration in the Pork Futures Warehouse?

3 What did the troll wearing a tutu and small gauze wings claim as his excuse for breaking and entering?

4 Who was thought unlikely to last long in the music business with a stage name like his?

5 Who wielded the dread weapon known as the Piecemaker?

6 The all-troll rock band was imaginatively called 'A Big Troll & . . .' what?

7 What, corresponding to the Mafia's dons, are the heavyweight leaders of the trollish Breccia called?

8 Hardcore was nailed to a wall by his ears for selling troll children bags of . . . what?

9 Whose teeth, according to a League member, were offensive to trolls?

10 What's the name of the troll night-club owned by the sinister Chryoprase?

11 Which Discworld musical features trolls in the title?

12 Which quip of Mae West's did provocative troll entertainer Ruby imitate with her badinage beginning, 'Is that the legendary Sceptre of Magma who was King of the Mountain . . .'?

Unseen University – The Sages of the Unknown Shadow

How's your general knowledge, wizards and sourcerers? More of those abbreviations, initials, codes, and symbols, with a hint of context to help your memory. (**Answers** on page 172.)

1 Academically: B.F.
2 Academically: BU.
3 Aviationally: BA.
4 Bibliographically: PONGO.
5 Cryptographically: in which Discworld text can we find a table of Messenger Pigeon Code examples? (GKB: The Alchemists' Guild has just exploded. GKBR: Now the wreckage of the Alchemists' Guild has just exploded . . .)
6 Dentally: form GV19.
7 Fractally: QWB.
8 Gastronomically: unofficial motto $\eta\beta\pi$.
9 Nominally: One-Man-Bucket.
10 Quizzically: TUUC.

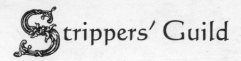

Strippers' Guild

This guild generally prefers to be called the guild of Ecdysiasts, Nautchers, Cancanières and Exponents of Exotic Dance. You are invited to tear away any veils of misdirection in the questions below, and reveal the naked truth. (**Answers** on page 174.)

1 What was the surname of Miss VaVa, who performed the acclaimed Feather Dance to the very last feather at the Skunk Club in *Soul Music*?

2 Whose promised exotic dance was rudely greeted by, 'How much do we have to pay for her not to?'

3 Who was unsurprised when a handsome young woman streaked past him in an alley and removed all her clothes?

4 What is special about a troll stripper's performance?

5 What disrupted the Dolly Sisters' Baking and Flower Circle, 'causing much Disarray of the Tarts before being Apprehended by the Trifles'?

6 Who refuted the suggestion that everyone is naked under their clothes, and how?

7 Where was the Mad Bishop of Pseudopolis killed, with fifteen naked maidens in attendance?

8 Who reclined on his couch at the top of the world, drinking lager and blackcurrent and surrounded by naked maenads?

9 Who, in the presence of a book revealing (with woodcuts) that the ladies of Slakki island wear no clothes at all and are of surpassing beauty, declared 'I'm sure none of us wish to know that'?

10 Which small reptiles unprotected by the Guild are cruelly misused in a related activity?

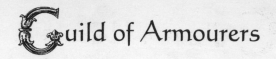

Guild of Armourers

Welcome to the storehouse of Discworld weaponry, ordnance, and boys' toys in general . . . (**Answers** on page 175.)

1 The 'Meteor' Automated Throwing Star Hurler (Decapitates at Twenty Paces) was sold with what money-back guarantee?

2 With what weapon, during a game of the gods, did the High Priest of the Green Robe do it in the library?

3 On what happy occasion do we encounter a Klatchian War Chariot with Real Spinning Sword Blades?

4 What incinerated most of the Omnian fleet?

5 Whose Protective broke the patella of an attacker who'd attempted a low blow?

6 What was the dread weapon wielded by Bh'rian Bloodaxe in the Battle of Koom Valley?

7 What Klatchian weapon looked like a very large kettle and had been banned by eight countries and three religions?

8 Who, in the season of festive gifts, yearned for a Burleigh and Stronginthearm double action triple-cantilever cross-bow?

9 What unorthodox weapon is most effective against Auditors of Reality when in human form?

10 What is the special interest of the Friendly Flamethrowers' League?

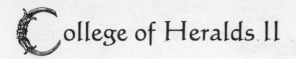

College of Heralds II

Another requirement for Heralds is wide expertise on the animals, real and mythical, which appear in coats of arms – or might one day. (**Answers** on page 176.)

1 What kind of creature, actually, is the morpork in Ankh-Morpork?

2 What unusual festive animals appeared on the wrapping paper of gifts provided by the stand-in Hogfather?

3 What useful current information can be read from the activities of the Hershebian lawyer beetle?

4 What, according to the mystic search engines of Death's library, are the harmless creatures of Fourecks?

5 Which household pest looked like a very small elephant with a very wide, flared trunk?

6 What useful future information can be read from the activities of the tree-climbing Burglar Crab?

7 In a famous painting by Leonard of Quirm, what animal is held by the woman considered to be the epitome of female beauty?

8 Where might one find black peacocks with a grim pattern replacing the 'eyes' in their tails?

9 What kind of animal was the poorly trained William, who walked into burrows and kicked the rabbits to death?

10 What, in the Shambles, did they call the treacherous 'employee' that led innocent beasts through the slaughterhouse door?

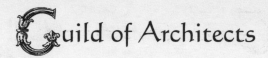

Guild of Architects

Buildings, constructions, habitations, edifices . . . have your theodolites at the ready! (**Answers** on page 177.)

1 Who lived in the Castle of Bones?

2 What Ankh-Morpork building was more than ten times as tall as Unseen University's Tower of Art?

3 What was the usual name for the contaminated magic dump just Hubwards of the university, on which the modern development Thaumatological Park was eventually built?

4 Which building in Whirligig Alley offered displays of combat muffins and throwing toast?

5 Harry Dread the Evil Dark Lord started his career with just two lads and – what modest headquarters?

6 Which imposing building is at the centre of the circular, onion-layered street plan of Ankh-Morpork?

7 What had an earthed copper roof as protection from angry gods, but was set ablaze anyway by a leading philosopher?

8 What is the present use of the former Palace de Tintemente in Ankh-Morpork, commonly called the Tanty?

9 Whose oriental palace was known as the Rhoxie?

10 Where could one find the Ankh-Morpork triumphal arch that commemorated the Battle of Crumhorn and incorporated over ninety statues of famous soldiers?

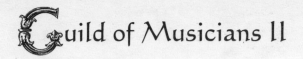uild of Musicians II

Again it's time to face the music. Take your time. (**Answers** on page 178.)

1 Whose what has a what on the end?

2 What Roundworld team is echoed by the dwarf songwriters Gorlick and Hammerjug?

3 Which city other than Ankh-Morpork is fiercely proud of its opera house?

4 What was wrong with Anaglypta Huggs's folksong 'The red rosy hen greets the dawn of day'?

5 In which other Guild had the unsympathetic Mr Clete worked just before advancing himself by a transfer to the Musicians?

6 Which ethnic group gave us the famous opera *Bloodaxe and Ironhammer*?

7 As the song of the great metropolis goes, 'Ankh-Morpork! Ankh-Morpork! So good they named it' – what?

8 What Roundworld song is suggested by Imp y Celyn's more or less Welsh title 'Sioni Bod Da'?

9 What song did dwarfs involved in the new industry of Holy Wood find themselves spontaneously singing?

10 Whose voice was trained for three years with Mme Venturi at the Quirm Conservatory?

$\mathscr{S}$mugglers' Guild

It is believed that this Guild is using L-space connections to smuggle in goods from other realities. In which Discworld novels can you find the equivalents or echoes of these Roundworld originals? (**Answers** on page 179.)

1 ELIZA the banal conversationalist: 'Tell me about your spoon.'

2 The 1994 movie *The Adventures of Priscilla, Queen of the Desert.*

3 The *Tomb Raider* game, with its convenient weapons, keys and medical packs strewn around the unexplored caverns.

4 Tiny Tim's exit line in Dickens.

5 Sir Frank Whittle, inventor of the jet engine.

6 The place where President John F. Kennedy's assassin stood, with related conspiracy theories.

7 Bernadotte, the French general who became, by invitation, crown prince and eventually king of Sweden (whose royal line had died out).

8 A. A. Milne's poem 'Lines and Squares' from *When We Were Very Young.*

9 The music hall sand-dancers Wilson, Keppel and Betty.

10 The Diet of Worms in 1521 (a meeting of the Diet or assembly of the Holy Roman Empire).

11 Benjamin Franklin's famous electrical experiment involving a thunderstorm and a kite.

12 The motto of the Los Angeles Police Department.

Guild of Cunning Artificers II

Below is a table of named Cunning Artifices from Discworld – devices, constructs, methods, codes, and so on. Match each one with its own use, from this list: autopilot, computation, devotional training, fisticuffs, game, housing and storage, observation, reading invisible writings, retrospective erasure, timekeeping. (**Answers** on page 181.)

1 Ajandurah's Wand of Utter Negativity.
2 The Barbarian Invaders Machine.
3 The Device of Erratic Balls.
4 The Phase of the Moon Generator.
5 Prince Haran's Tiller.
6 The Make-Things-Bigger Device.
7 The Marquis of Fantailler Rules.
8 The Ornamental Cruet Set of Mad Lord Snapcase.
9 Weezencake's Unreliable Algorithm.
10 Wheelbright's Gravity Escapement.

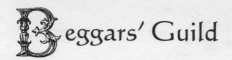

Beggars' Guild

For the sake of unreasonable complexity and mystification, this heading also covers street people whom even the Beggars are rather embarrassed about and have considered running out of town. (**Answers** on page 183.)

1 Which bridge of Ankh-Morpork did its best-known and seediest group of street people live beneath?

2 Who joined the just-mentioned group and was known as Mr Scrub?

3 Why does it seem paradoxical that Arnold Sideways should stick his boot in a door to keep it open?

4 Who was a 'physical schizophrenic' whose other half could arrive in places before he did and cause people's ear wax to melt?

5 Who said, 'You couldn't spare I ten thousand dollars for a small mansion, could you?'?

6 Jossi, Lady Hermione, Little Sidney, Cumbling Michael, Mr Viddle, Curly, the Judge, Tinker and Burke: who's the odd one out?

7 Sidney Lopsides was so disconcerting in appearance that he was paid two dollars a day from City funds to – what?

8 Who was famed for his expertise at producing a cough that sounded almost solid?

9 Who provided thinking-brain services to the afflicted?

10 Which Discworld character first uttered that well-known street catchphrase 'Millennium hand and shrimp'?

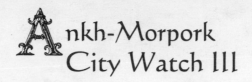

Ankh-Morpork City Watch III

Yet another challenge to trainee Watchmen: can you spot the suspicious character or item that's the odd one out in each of these lists? (**Answers** on page 184.)

1. Annually: Assassins, Butchers, Fools, Thieves, Watch, Wizards.
2. Aurientally: Fang, Hong, Hunghung, McSweeney, Sung, Tang.
3. Cartographically: Anger, Bestiality, Catastrophe, Covetousness, Deviousness, Dread, Jealousy.
4. Ceramically: Bobkes, Dibbuk, Dorfl, Klutz, Knurd, Shmata.
5. Honorifically: Clarissa Extendo, Violetta Gigli, Margyreen Glazier, Janeen Ormulu, Sybil Ramkin, Wendy Sackville.
6. Marshily: Birbright's Smut, Curly-Maned Slottie, Smooth Deceiver, Spiked Oncer, Tabby Cowper, Unstirring Divisor.
7. Politically: Lord Harmoni, Lord Rust, Lord Snapcase, Lord Vetinari, Lord Winder.
8. Porcinely: Gouger, Rooter, Slasher, Snouter, Tusker.
9. Quadruply: Denial, Gossip, Misinformation, Panic, Rumour.
10. Ritually: figgin, gaskin, moules, tridlins, welchet.

Fine Art Appreciation Society

Let us stroll amid the splendours of Discworld art, past masterpieces like Caravati's Three Large Pink Women and One Piece of Gauze, *and sharpen our critical senses.* (**Answers** on page 186.)

1 What painting by Leonard of Quirm, echoing an utterly famous Roundworld portrait but with a witchy twist, had teeth that followed you around the room?

2 Which feature of Leonard of Quirm's *Woman Holding Ferret* followed you around the room?

3 The painting of Rincewind fleeing across a little bridge from a pursuing crowd in the wooded garden had to be simplified, and there was only blue paint left . . . suggesting what famous Roundworld design?

4 Who drew a complex allegorical picture of a crowned figure made up of many smaller figures?

5 Who was the distinguished, grey-haired man who in his portrait is wearing evening dress and the sash and star of the Order of Gvot?

6 Which cold-blooded artist who specialized in fern designs tried his hand (after criticism) at three little dogs looking out of a boot, an Auriental lady and a vase of sunflowers?

7 What resulted from the wizards' argument about how exactly one should draw a duck?

8 Who made sketches of the lost land of Leshp before it was actually found?

9 What ingenious facsimile of an ancient original was smuggled out of Ankh-Morpork in the ambassador's coach?

10 Where was there a picture of a brown stag being attacked by brown dogs on a brown moorland against an improbable brown sky?

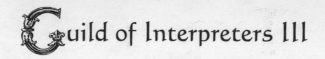

Guild of Interpreters III

More translation tasks: unravel these phrases from Latatian and other arcane Discworld tongues. (**Answers** on page 187.)

1. Dwarfish: 'Let's hang them up by the *bura'zak-ka!*' (A kind of punishment not practised in Ankh-Morpork.)
2. Pictogram: urinating dog.
3. Nac mac Feeglish: 'imhoe'.
4. *Torquus Simiae Maleficarum.*
5. The pets' beauty salon: *Le Poil de Chien.*
6. Dwarfish (the name of a Discworld regular): *Sh'rt'azs.*
7. Legalese: *Acquiris Quodcumque Rapis.*
8. Restaurant Quirmian: *Mousse de la Boue dans une Panier de la Pâte de Chaussures.*
9. Nac mac Feeglish: ''yin, tan, TETRA!'
10. DICO, DICO, DICO.
11. Hex card: two round holes, then a whole pattern of round holes, and then a further two holes.
12. Dwarfish: 'the way you *krazak* your *G'ardrgh.*'

The Opera House

An easy one for opera-lovers!!!!! Complete the Discworld opera or musical titles below, using each of the following words or fragments just once: Hita, Horse, La, Leiv, Les, Piccolo, Pseudopolis, Truccatore, Scrote, Shaak. Give the equivalent Roundworld opera titles. (**Answers** on page 188.)

1 *The Barber of* . . .

2 *Cosi fan* . . .

3 *Die Fleder* . . .

4 *Die Meistersinger von* . . .

5 *The Enchanted* . . .

6 *Il* . . .

7 *Lohen* . . .

8 *Miserable* . . .

9 *The Student* . . . (including the famous song 'Ich Bin Ein Rattarsedschwein')

10 . . . *Triviata.*

Thieves' Guild II

Further questions concerning shady characters, characters from the Shades, and those fine upstanding citizens of the Guild. (**Answers** on page 189.)

1 Section Two, Rule One of the Thieves' Guild Charter says that members must on all professional occasions carry – what?

2 Who grew up in Rookery Yard in the Shades, sharing a drain ('We thought people in gutters were *nobs*') with two other families and a man who juggled eels?

3 Whose test required him to recognize a complex rune that, *if it were the other way up*, would be thiefsign for 'Noisy dogs in this house'?

4 Who was the brains of that sinister criminal organization the New Firm?

5 Who reckoned that when her relative Nev nicked the lead off the Opera House roof, it wasn't the same as *stealing*?

6 'Who streals my prurse streals trasph,' says a drunkenly slurred Nobby in *Feet of Clay* – mangling a famous line spoken by which character in Shakespeare?

7 The inept thief Here'n'Now, according to *The Discworld Companion*, is so called because he speaks only in the present tense – reflecting the peculiar style of which Roundworld author's stories about underworld characters?

8 Third-class thief Mooty Zebbo intended a routine coshing but instead died very suddenly in a way no one had died for hundreds of years – how?

9 What gigantic theft was masterminded by the mild-mannered former teacher Ronald Saveloy?

10 Who planned to climb Dunmanifestin to steal the Secret of Fire from the gods, only to discover this had in fact been done thousands of years before?

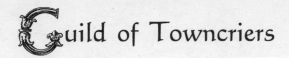

Guild of Towncriers

*The following memorable cries, or at any rate lines of dialogue, are cried or at any rate spoken by Discworld characters. Though sometimes slightly mangled, they all have a Roundworld origin. Name the original authors or publications. (**Answers** on page 190.)*

1 The Patrician in *The Fifth Elephant*: 'Uberwald remains a mystery inside a riddle wrapped in an enigma.'

2 Carrot navigating: 'Second star to the left and straight on 'til morning.'

3 Nobby to Colon: 'We're all lyin' in the gutter, Fred. But some of us're lookin' at the stars . . .'

4 Susan: '. . . *yes*, Twyla, there *is* a Hogfather.'

5 Lady Margolotta: 'Go and tell the children of the night to make vonderful music somevhere else . . .'

6 Dorfl the golem: 'Somewhere, A Crime Is Happening.'

7 Count de Magpyr on vampire self-improvement: 'Every day, in every way, we get better and better . . .'

8 Embarrassed Ankh-Morpork street gangs: 'Wob wob wob.'

9 Carrot: 'We can rebuild him. We have the pottery.'

10 The Horned King to the Elf Queen: Something about meeting by moonlight.

Minor Guilds and Societies III

There are high-flying guilds and societies, and then again there are lesser ones like the Bandits, Launderers and Smugglers. Here we go again! (**Answers** on page 192.)

1 Which society met three doors down the street from the Illuminated and Ancient Brethren of Ee?

2 What is the invariable surname given to orphans and foundlings brought up by the Clockmaker's Guild?

3 Which Discworld organization sang rousing songs like 'Steady Progress and Limited Disobedience While Retaining Well-Formulated Good Manners'?

4 Who is the only known member of the Ankh-Morpork Folk-Dance and Song Club?

5 Which Guild awards the Golden Mallet for the largest catch each year?

6 What is the focus of the *other* Cavern Club, the one that shouldn't be confused with the troll night-club?

7 Silas Cumberbatch, formerly of the Towncriers' Guild, is a Watch member in *Men at Arms*. What is the Roundworld significance of his name?

8 Which devout group's members make long journeys to place small brass weights on otherwise unremarkable mountains and islets?

9 The female leaders of four guilds supported Lord Vetinari at a difficult time in *The Truth*: the Beggars, Exotic Dancers, Seamstresses and . . . which other?

10 Where did Mr Saveloy teach geography for a few terms after doing so at the Assassins' and Plumbers' Guilds?

Philosophers' Tavern III

Yet more proverbial philosophy – well-known phrases, sayings and old saws in their mangled Discworld incarnations. Fill in the missing words indicated by XXXX ... (**Answers** on page 193.)

1 'Give a man a fire and he's warm for a day, but XXXX XXXX XXXX XXXX and he's warm for the rest of his life.'

2 As they say in Omnia, 'If XXXX XXXX XXXX won't go to the mountain, the mountain must go to XXXX XXXX XXXX.'

3 '*Now* we're cooking with XXXX.'

4 'Never trust a wizard over XXXX–XXXX.'

5 'Walk a mile on these XXXX.'

6 Reg Shoe on the soapbox: '. . . let me say, we shall not lie back and let the grass grow XXXX XXXX XXXX.'

7 Ridcully on evolution: 'Survival of the XXXXest.'

8 Carrot: 'I feel it is the XXXX before the Storm . . .'

9 Vimes: 'Been there, done that, bought the XXXX . . .'

10 'Nanny Ogg says you must take time by the XXXX.'

The History Monks

In theory, the History Monks keep Discworld events moving along their allotted course – and hence these questions about historical or legendary events of long ago. (**Answers** on page 194.)

1 Who carried out the same complex and rigidly observed daily rituals for 7,000 years?

2 What kind of mining had been forbidden in Uberwald since the Diet of Bugs in AM 1880?

3 What jealously guarded secret did the troll folk-hero Monolith steal from the gods?

4 What forgotten thoroughfare carried the inscription *Cirone IV me fabricat*, indicating it was built in the reign of an early king more than 2,000 years previously?

5 Which impressive event of long ago was immediately criticized with the words 'Too showy. You don't need all that noise.'?

6 What was the source of the very special iron from which the 'standing stones' called the Dancers were made?

7 Which god's sacred text, or at least its Apocrypha, was the only known holy book to contain the phrase 'Take that you bastard we've been waiting ages to get you for what you did all those years ago'?

8 Who founded Unseen University approximately 2,000 years before the current Discworld 'present'?

9 Who were the opposing sides in the historical Battle of Koom Valley?

10 Where, since its founding, was there always cherry blossom?

Unseen University: The Last Order, or The Other Order

According to an immemorial tradition established on this very page, the Last Order of Wizardry provides the last set of questions and tries to make them extra difficult. Take a deep breath . . . (**Answers** on page 195.)

1 Which name for a ship of the Circle Sea distantly echoes Christopher Columbus's *Pinta*? (Clue: the answer is not *The Prid of Ankh-Morpork*.)

2 What is the special significance – to a limited group – of 'William Rubin' as a little boy's name in *Hogfather*?

3 Which Discworld novel first pointed out that teeth taken by the Tooth Fairy could be magically used to control children?

4 Which Roundworld poet is being echoed when Mr Sock the butcher thinks of his golem as a 'damned two-handed engine'?

5 Which eccentric reference book first published in 1870 appeared in an expanded Millennium Edition with an introduction by Terry Pratchett?

6 Who, rowing on a foul-smelling stream, said: 'Just call me King of the Golden River, eh?'

7 Terry Pratchett reckoned that 'I can best repay their kindness by not mentioning their names here'. What strange help had these people given him?

8 For those with *really* good memories: which ancient and truly original order of wizardry has not featured in any previous quiz paper or answer in this book?

9 In which non-Discworld novel was 'famine' a seven-letter word?

10 Which Discworld character says his surname is spelt with an O although it doesn't contain one?

11 What is *Ninox novaeseelandiae*?

12 What is or was *Psephophorus terrypratchetti*?

Answers

Guild of Fools
and Joculators

Questions on page 7

1 'A full dozen at cock-crow, and something less under the dog-star, by reason of the dew, which lies heavy on men taken by the scurvy.' Non-Fool answer: Discworld novel number three, *Equal Rites*.

2 'If he be right astronomically, then is he the greater dunce in respect of true learning, the which goes by the globe. Argal, 'twere better he widened his wind-pipe.' Non-Fool answer: Rincewind. See *The Light Fantastic*.

3 'Argal, I stick at nothing but cobble-stones, which by the same token, are stuck to the road by men's fingers.' Non-Fool answer: Boiled slugs. See *Men at Arms*.

4 'With a nid, and a nod, and a niddy-niddy-o.' Non-Fool answer: Archchancellor Galder Weatherwax in *The Light Fantastic*; his connection to Granny Weatherwax is confirmed in *Lords and Ladies*.

5 'I am for Lancaster, and that's to say, for good shoe leather.' Non-Fool answer: Muddy old boots. See *Hogfather*.

6 'I'faith, nuncle, thou't more full of questions than a martlebury is of mizzensails.' Non-Fool answer: 'What is your name?' This was the special Unseen University exam set in *Moving Pictures* to force eternal student Victor Tugelbend into graduating (or failing utterly).

7 'I did impeticos thy gratility; for Malvolio's nose is no whipstock.' Non-Fool answer: High Priest Dios, the effective ruler of the land of Djelibeybi in *Pyramids*.

8 'Thou art not so long by the head as honorificabilitudinitatibus; thou art easier swallowed than a flap-dragon.' Non-

Fool answer: Short Street. See in particular the Mapp in *The Streets of Ankh-Morpork*.

9 'If a man's brains were in's heels, were't not in danger of kibes?' Non-Fool answer: Laddie in *Moving Pictures*.

10 'It is like a barber's chair that fits all buttocks: the pin-buttock, the quatch-buttock, the brawn-buttock, or any buttock.' Non-Fool answer: *Feet of Clay*, in which this admirable summary is recited by Dorfl the golem. The first two directives come from *Robocop*, but not the third.

Bonus question: which of the Foolish answers above actually comes from a Discworld novel? All but one are by other authors, including Shakespeare. (See Extra Answers, page 199.)

The Lancre Witches

Questions on page 8

1 Granny Weatherwax wins. The main actual interest is in which other witch manages to come second. (*A Tourist Guide to Lancre*, 'The Sea and Little Fishes')

2 Mrs Gogol in *Witches Abroad*. They may call it voodoo over there in Genua, but it's still what they call witchcraft in Lancre.

3 Agnes Nitt, whose inner thin girl was called Perdita. (*Carpe Jugulum*)

4 Granny Weatherwax, as revealed in *Maskerade*. Her conclusion: 'Never pick yourself a name you can't scrub the floor in.'

5 Nanny Ogg, in *Thief of Time*.

6 Magrat Garlick, in *Witches Abroad*. **Bonus question:** which witch was godmother to *her* child? (See Extra Answers, page 199.)

7 Warts, 'a face like a sockful of marbles', giving real crone-credibility. Granny was never able to grow any warts. (*Equal Rites*)

8 Nanny Ogg having a bath, and singing in it. People cowered indoors and under tables at the sound of her high C. (*Lords and Ladies*)

9 Agnes/Perdita Nitt, who ended the opera in *Maskerade* with a cry that devastatingly spanned the entire audible spectrum. 'It isn't over until the fat lady sings . . .'

10 Magrat Garlick in her highly practical travelling trousers. (*Witches Abroad*)

Offler's League of Temperance

Questions on page 9

1 Bibulous, God of Wine, in *Hogfather*.

2 Bearhugger's Very Fine Whisky, Samuel Vimes's former drink of choice. (*Guards! Guards!*, *Men at Arms*, etc.)

3 War, in *Thief of Time*.

4 Bull's Blood – metaphorically in Hungary, literally in Discworld. (*The Fifth Elephant*)

5 With counterwise wine made from magic reannual grapes, you get the hangover or hangunder before actually drinking it. (*Pyramids*)

6 Embalming fluid, perhaps one reason why Mr Slant – a zombie – was so well preserved. (*The Truth*)

7 Lord Downey, head of the Assassins' Guild in *Hogfather*. Backwards labels are supposed to confuse the servant classes, who according to a Pratchett footnote may respond by topping up the Yksihw bottle with eniru.

8 Scumble – these are Discworld varieties of apple. (*The Discworld Companion*) **Bonus question:** which of these is linked with the name 'Drum'? (See Extra Answers, page 199.)

9 Coffee, which had got out of hand when a party of wizards excited by Music With Rocks In had decided it ought to be frothy. (*Soul Music*)

10 A Bloody Mary. (*Hogfather*)

Guild of Engravers

Questions on page 10

1 *Men at Arms* – motto inscribed on the Ankh-Morpork Post Office. **Bonus question:** which real-world building carries the better spelt inscription echoed by this motto? (See Extra Answers, page 199.)

2 *Thief of Time* – the warning sign displayed by the Death of Rats' ingenious mechanical malignity detector.

3 *Moving Pictures* – the hard-hitting movie poster for the romantic tragedy (in two reels) of *Pelias and Melisande*. 'With a 1,000 elephants!'

4 *Guards! Guards!* – the 2000 comic book adaptation by Graham Higgins and Stephen Briggs. Another typically colourful fragment of Ankh-Morpork street culture.

5 *The Science of Discworld* – the hypothetical sign which, if placed on a guillotine, wizards of Unseen University would be quite likely to disobey.

6 *Carpe Jugulum* – poster pinned outside the Quite Reverend Mightily Oats's mission tent in Lancre.

7 *The Truth* – sign carried by street person Coffin Henry. Half a mark for guessing any other member of Foul Ole Ron's band, such as the Duck Man, Coffin Henry, Arnold Sideways, or Ron himself.

8 *Interesting Times* – inscription on the tomb of the legendary One Sun Mirror, founder of the Agatean Empire.

9 *Thief of Time* – a sign put up in Ankh-Morpork's Royal Art Museum in order to confuse the very literal-minded Auditors of Reality.

10 *Moving Picture* – the wizards' city map correctly marks Lady Sybil Ramkin's Sunshine Sanctuary for Sick Dragons with this label. The sign on the Sanctuary itself reads HERE BE DRAGNS. (*Men at Arms*)

Minor Guilds
and Societies

Questions on page 11

1 Gaspode the Wonder Dog, the notorious talking dog of Ankh-Morpork urban myth, proves also to be a writing dog in *The Fifth Elephant*.

2 The Elucidated Brethren of the Ebon Night, very shortly before the dragon came calling in *Guards! Guards!*

3 The Ankh-Morpork Caged Birds Society, in *The Truth*.

4 During Sergeant (Acting Captain) Colon's disastrous management of the Watch in *The Fifth Elephant*. 'Colon! Colon! Colon! Out! Out! Out!' **Bonus question:** Why did Nobby Nobbs think 'That doesn't sound right . . .'? (See Extra Answers, page 199.)

5 Draught excluders for the windier parts of Lancre castle. (*Carpe Jugulum*)

6 They turn the handles of clicks (movie) cameras, continually bringing new frames of octo-cellulose into place for the next picture to be painted, and also lashing on the tiny imps who do the painting. (*Moving Pictures*)

7 'Shave and a haircut, no legs.' (*Carpe Jugulum*)

8 The Thieves' Guild; Ludd's Lads and Lasses, named for a guild founder, are abandoned children adopted into and raised by the guild. (*Thief of Time*)

9 The city's golems, as noted in *The Truth*.

10 In the introduction to *The Science of Discworld*.

The Librarians of
Time and Space

Questions on page 13

1 Evelyn Waugh also wrote a novel called *Men at Arms*, published in 1952.

2 'We don't want to fight, but, by *Jingo!* if we do, We've got the ships, we've got the men, we've got the money too.' Or as the Patrician more dourly and accurately rephrases it in the novel: 'We have no ships. We have no men. We have no money, too.'

3 *Interesting Times*.

4 Salieri, Mozart's sworn enemy in *Amadeus*, has a name meaning 'seller of salt'; in *Maskerade* the musical director of the Ankh-Morpork Opera House is – all together now – Salzella.

5 The retina of a dead man's eye – producing an image of the last thing he saw in life. (The trick doesn't in fact work in our world, but Discworld rules are different . . .)

6 Seattle, Washington State, America – as identified in the Author's Note at the beginning of *The Truth*.

7 Peach Melba, named for the Australian coloratura soprano Dame Nellie Melba. **Bonus question:** where did the Butt in Dame Nellie Butt come from? (See Extra Answers, page 199.)

8 Once up a time in the 1930s there was a *News Chronicle* newspaper promotion in which anyone spotting their agent 'Lobby Lud' at pre-announced seaside resorts could win a prize by accosting him. When the *Daily Mirror* later imitated the campaign, the formula 'You are Lobby Lud and I claim my five pounds!' became a national catchphrase. When young Newgate Ludd joins the History Monks in *Thief of Time*, he becomes Lobsang Ludd.

9 One dubious theory of Napoleon's death is that he was poisoned by arsenical fumes from the green (arsenic-dyed) wallpaper in his room. In *Feet of Clay*, Vimes wonders at length about the horrible green wallpaper of the Patrician's room. . . .

10 The very first novel in Leslie Charteris's 'Saint' thriller series was also called *The Last Hero* when published in 1930. Eleven years later, just to make this question trickier, it was retitled *The Saint Closes the Case*.

Ankh-Morpork
City Watch

Questions on page 15

1 Only the *Mort* comic contains no drawings by the multi-talented Stephen 'Mr Ubiquitous' Briggs.

2 'Bloody stupid elements . . . fall to bits as soon as you look at them' formed in Unseen University's Roundworld Project in *The Science of Discworld* and named after wizards (Bursar, Lecturer in Recent Runes, Senior Wrangler) – except for cohenium, from co-author Jack Cohen. Or was it Cohen the Barbarian? Not a wizard, anyway . . .

3 Igor's former mad scientist employers are cited in *Thief of Time*, with the exception of Psychoneurotic (or sometimes just plain Mad) Lord Snapcase, a past Patrician of Ankh-Morpork who's mentioned in *Guards! Guards!* and *Men at Arms*.

4 Bes Pelargic is the chief port of the far-off Agatean Empire; the other places are all in Uberwald. (Or Überwald, if you prefer umlauts.)

5 Rains of all these objects are mentioned in *Jingo*. However, the chocolate biscuits don't fall in sceptical modern times but only in Omnian scriptures quoted by Constable Visit.

6 These are exotic martial arts, genuine or made-up, mentioned in a conversation in *Thief of Time* – except for the puzuma (properly the Ambiguous Puzuma), a rare Discworld animal.

7 All heart-warming, fattening, stick-to-your-ribs Ankh-Morpork dishes, except for the suspiciously foreign squishi – identified in the *Companion* as 'possibly like sushi, only older'.

8 All these creatures came spontaneously into being as a result of belief. Four appear in *Hogfather*, accidentally created by wizards in a time of worldwide surplus belief. The exception is the Dragon of Unhappiness from *The Truth*, conjured up as a side effect of C.M.O.T. Dibbler's all too persuasive marketing of Fung Shooey. **Bonus question:** what subtle rearrangement of household furniture had he prescribed? (See Extra Answers, page 200.)

9 This is an undead question. Mr Slant the lawyer (various books), Windle Poons (after his death in *Reaper Man*), Reg Shoe (*Reaper Man* and later books) and Baron Saturday (*Witches Abroad*) were or are zombies; the exception is the Count de Magpyr from *Carpe Jugulum*, a vampire.

10 Various unsavoury afflictions of Gaspode the Wonder Dog as listed in *The Fifth Elephant* – the exception being slab throat, a disease of swamp dragons. Which isn't to say that Gaspode mightn't catch it one day.

Philosophers' Tavern

Questions on page 16

1 A is 'musicians' and B is 'hat'. (*Soul Music*)

2 C is 'vulture'. (*Pyramids*)

3 D is 'scalbies'. (*Small Gods*)

4 E is 'ravens'. Scalbies are stated in *Small Gods* to be members of the crow family.

5 F is 'Ankh-Morpork'. (*Moving Pictures*)

6 G is 'the colour of magic'. (*The Colour of Magic*, first Discworld novel.)

7 H is 'octarine'. (Discworld *passim*.)

8 I is 'Death'. (*Reaper Man*) Actually I is David Langford, but you knows what I means.

9 J is 'rats'. (*Maskerade*)

10 K is 'vampire'. (*The Truth*)

11 L is 'dwarf'. (*The Fifth Elephant*)

12 M is 'troll'. (Discworld *passim*, especially *Men at Arms*)

13 N is 'elephant'. (*Soul Music*)

14 O is 'earthquake'. (*Moving Pictures*) **Bonus question:** what did the real-world Chinese device have in place of elephants? (See Extra Answers, page 200.)

15 A – as already noted – is 'musicians'; the reference is to Unseen University's organ. (*The Discworld Companion*, although it's suggested in *Maskerade* that the Librarian may break this rule.)

Guild of Interpreters

Questions on page 17

1 Presumably, 'crapped on from a great height' or something similar – the shield of the Vimes family, discredited for regicide. (*Feet of Clay*)

2 Werewolf family motto meaning 'Every man is a wolf to another man.' (*The Fifth Elephant*)

3 Nanny Ogg's tactful way of offering around the canapés in *Carpe Jugulum*.

4 Rincewind translates his motto for a dangerous mission in *The Last Hero*: 'We who are about to die don't want to.'

5 The motto on the baker's arms: Because I Knead The Dough. (*Feet of Clay*)

6 The honorary degree Doctor of Sweet Fanny Adams (i.e., bugger all), as awarded in *Jingo*.

7 A werewolf – by birth and blood – that can't change but remains fixed in human or wolf form. (*The Fifth Elephant*)

8 'No Worries' – motto of the Unseen University of Bugarup, XXXX, in *The Last Continent*. **Bonus question:** translate the graffito on this edifice's wall, reading *Nulli Sheilae sanguineae*. (See Extra Answers, page 200.)

9 'Don't Fear the Reaper' – a Blue Oyster Cult song title, and also the motto of the Duchy of Sto Helit, i.e. Mort and Ysabell in *Mort* and their daughter Susan. (*Hogfather*) Probably it should be *timetis* rather than *temetis*.

10 'This damn' door sticks,' according to the translation in *Maskerade*.

11 Rincewind's favourite incantation: 'Oh shit, oh shit, oh shit . . .' Continuing with *moriturus sum*, 'I'm going to die.' (*Interesting Times*)

12 Bit of a trick question, this. On Discworld, Pencillium – in full, Osric Pencillium – had nothing to do with antibiotics but discovered, in the graphite-rich sands of Sumtri, a bush which yielded the writing implement named after him. (*Hogfather*)

The Hoodwinkers

Questions on page 18

1 A pair of corroded boots, rather than the typical Oxbridge oar. It is necessary to run rather than row over the surface of the Ankh river. (*Interesting Times*)

2 'Not this bit.' (*The Science of Discworld*)

3 Rincewind, as contemplated by Death in *The Last Continent*. **Bonus question:** who actually wrote that mythological study *The Hero With a Thousand Faces*? (See Extra Answers, page 200.)

4 Ponder Stibbons, youngest member of the current faculty: Reader since *Lord and Ladies*, Head in *The Last Hero*.

5 Rincewind, in *The Science of Discworld*; he's still in this post, though unpaid, in *The Last Hero*.

6 The Bursar – although we don't learn his surname until *Hogfather* or his initials and titles until *The Truth*.

7 The Dean, notably in *Reaper Man*, where it became quite catching.

8 Coin, the Sourcerer, in *Sourcery*.

9 Rincewind, as reassured by Stibbons in *Interesting Times*. The line appeared on movie posters for the 1986 remake of *The Fly*.

10 'Numbers' Riktor, creator of other useful devices like the resograph and the Swamp Meter. (*Moving Pictures*)

Guild of Teachers

Questions on page 20

1 In response to the universal prayers of teachers, the Guild clock strikes the hour early. (*Men at Arms*)

2 That it is impossible to fall off them. (*Soul Music*)

3 'Good heavens, all of 4B?' (*Interesting Times*)

4 Wen's apprentice Clodpool, in *Thief of Time*.

5 The requirement was to name three poisons acknowledged for administration by ear. Any paraphrase will do! (*Pyramids*)

6 William de Worde, in *The Truth*.

7 The de Magpyr family of vampires in *Carpe Jugulum*. **Bonus question:** what phobia was treated by this exposure to holy symbols? (See Extra Answers, page 200.)

8 One gold star was worth three silver ones. (*The Thief of Time*)

9 Unseen University, Ankh-Morpork. The Ancient and Truly Original Brothers of the Silver Star is one of the eight orders of wizardry. (*Equal Rites*)

10 The Assassins' Guild school. (*Assassins' Guild Yearbook and Diary 2000*)

Guild of Actors
and Mummers

Questions on page 21

1 Edward d'Eath in *Men at Arms*, as part of his devious plot to steal a deadly weapon from the Assassins' Guild.

2 Charlie, former keeper of a clothes shop in Pseudopolis, who is unfortunate enough to be a dead ringer for the Patrician in *The Truth*.

3 Cohen the Barbarian and the Silver Horde (including Mr Saveloy, who fervently hopes the others won't realize they're disguised as eunuchs) in *Interesting Times*.

4 Twoflower becomes his Earthly analogue Zweiblumen (German for two flowers) when he and Rincewind (who becomes Dr Rjinswand) are briefly displaced into our own world in *The Colour of Magic*.

5 Magrat Garlick, former witch and queen-to-be of Lancre, is inspired by wearing Queen Ynci's armour in *Lords and Ladies*.

6 Chaos or Kaos, fifth horseman of the Discworld apocalypse, is revealed in *Thief of Time* to have been in hiding as the subtly surnamed milkman Ron Soak.

7 Almost all the senior wizards in *Moving Pictures*, while playing truant to visit the movies with their real beards cunningly disguised as false ones. You are allowed to feel smug if you actually named any of: the Chair of Indefinite Studies, the Lecturer in Recent Runes, the Dean, or Windle Poons – though *not* Archchancellor Ridcully, the Bursar, or the recently graduated Ponder Stibbons.

8 Death in seasonal midwinter guise, in *Hogfather*.

9 Lettice Knibbs, lady's maid to Queen Molly – shot in error while trying on the queen's cloak in *Men at Arms*. Take a

full point for 'maid' or 'lady's maid' even if you didn't recall her name. **Bonus question:** the velvet cloak or gown is prescribed by the Beggars' Guild Charter, quoted by Carrot in the book. What's the source of this? (See Extra Answers, page 200.)

10 Nobby Nobbs of the City Watch, having drawn the short straw when he, the Patrician and Sergeant Colon acquired the clothes of the Klatchian entertainers Gulli, Gulli and Beti in *Jingo*.

Guild of Merchants
and Traders

Questions on page 22

1 The tanners, in *The Truth*. Their use of the particularly repellent substance 'pure' – mentioned under another name in this novel – was documented in 1851 by Roundworld's amateur sociologist Henry Mayhew. **Bonus question:** what exactly is this stuff? (See Extra Answers, page 201.)

2 Musical instruments, most or all of them suspiciously magical, in *Soul Music*.

3 William Sonky, mentioned in *The Fifth Elephant*. A packet of Sonkies for the weekend, sir?

4 Dirty postcards. (*Jingo*)

5 The Mk II Dis-Organizer, a magical personal organizer with a host of useful features and a wide range of interesting and amusing sounds. (*The Truth*)

6 Holy water, with which a vampire employee has an accident in *Feet of Clay*.

7 Mrs Marietta Cosmopilite of 3 Quirm Street, Ankh-Morpork. (*Moving Pictures, Witches Abroad, Thief of Time*)

8 Cohen the Barbarian, alias Ghenghiz Cohen, in *Interesting Times*. He subsequently lapsed into character by attacking the apple merchant, setting fire to his stall and stealing all the money, but he *did* pay for the apple.

9 News and gossip, in circular letters composed by the industrious William de Worde. (*The Truth*)

10 *Wellcome to Ankh-Morpork, Citie of One Thousand Surprises*, mentioned in several Discworld novels. Have a mark for getting close even if your spelling wasn't rigorously inaccurate.

The Order of Midnight

Questions on page 23

1 Bonza Charlie's Beaut Sieve, we learn in *The Last Continent*, is the XXXX wizards' equivalent of the 'unmixing' spell known to Unseen University as Maxwell's Impressive Separator. It will separate, for example, sugar from sand. Perhaps wizards spill a lot of sugar. ‑

2 Gindle's Effortless Elevator. (*Moving Pictures*)

3 Sumpjumper's Incendiary Surprise. (*Reaper Man*)

4 Phandaal's Mantle of Stealth – this is the promised non-Discworld spell. It comes from Jack Vance's *The Dying Earth* (1950), to which the other spell names are Pratchett's gentle homage.

5 Stacklady's Morphic Resonator, useful for turning miscreants into pumpkins, as demonstrated in *Lords and Ladies*. **Bonus question:** who cast this spell? (See Extra Answers, page 201.)

6 Atavaar's Personal Gravitational Upset. (*The Colour of Magic*)

7 Brother Hushmaster's Potent Asp-Spray. (*Sourcery*)

8 Eringya's Surprising Bouquet. (*Reaper Man*)

9 Heisenberg's Uncertainty Principle – no, not a non–Discworld interloper but named after the wizard Sangrit Heisenberg, according to a footnote in *Interesting Times*.

10 Fresnel's Wonderful Concentrator – a sly allusion to the real-world Fresnel lens often used in stage lighting. (*The Colour of Magic*)

Guild of Musicians

Questions on page 24

1 'Don't Cry for Me, Genua' in *Maskerade*.

2 The Guild's short way with unlicensed music-players (in *Soul Music*) is to take their instruments and shove them somewhere carefully unspecified. 'It's not much fun for the piccolo player' – nor, we're told, for the trombonist.

3 To time a boiling egg, according to Granny Weatherwax in *Carpe Jugulum*.

4 A subtle but intentional reference to a line in Don McLean's song 'American Pie': 'In a coat he borrowed from James Dean . . .' Another line made famous by this song, 'the day the music died', is quoted earlier in *Soul Music*.

5 Fondel, author of the noted *Wedding March* and *Prelude in G Major*. (*Men at Arms*, *Soul Music*) **Bonus question:** which Discworld notable who didn't care to play or listen to Fondel's *Prelude* still enjoyed the austere pleasure of reading the score? (See Extra Answers, page 201.)

6 'Mrs Widgery's Lodger'; one wizards' order is Mrs Widgery's Lodgers. (*The Discworld Companion*)

7 'The Hedgehog Song', Nanny Ogg's favourite: 'The hedgehog can never be buggered at all.' Although she'd never admit it, Granny is wrong to call this insectivorous mammal a rodent. (*Witches Abroad*)

8 Hex, the Unseen University computer. (*The Last Continent*)

9 Having to help him find his fingers afterwards. Zombies really shouldn't play the guitar. (*Reaper Man*)

10 In the main hall of Don'tgonearthe Castle, family home of the de Magpyrs. (*Carpe Jugulum*)

Thieves' Guild

Questions on page 25

1 'Whip it quick.' (*The Discworld Companion*)

2 Banjo Lilywhite, in *Hogfather*.

3 Carrot, while still a very new and inexperienced Watchman, in *Guards! Guards!*

4 Newgate Ludd, in *Thief of Time*. He became Lobsang Ludd after a career change, but only half a point here if you identified him as Lobsang.

5 The Seamstresses, who are not quite what their name implies.

6 It consists of a real, dead thief turning gently in the wind. **Bonus question:** what was the point of this grisly display? (See Extra Answers, page 201.)

7 The name Fingers. Among the Elucidated Brethren of the Ebon Night, Boggis was known as Brother Fingers. (*Guards! Guards!*)

8 Banjo Lilywhite, in *Hogfather*.

9 Guild of Lags members will serve other people's prison sentences for an agreed fee. (*Discworld Thieves' Guild Yearbook and Diary 2002*)

10 Al-Ybi. (*The Discworld Companion*)

Guild of Accountants

Questions on page 26

1 Agatean Empire cash comes in gold *rhinu* and half-*rhinu* coins, echoing a bygone English slang word for money: 'rhino'. (*The Colour of Magic, Interesting Times*)

2 Djelibeybi's currency unit is the talent. 'Limestone at two talents the ton,' says a pyramid-builder in *Pyramids*.

3 Ephebe uses *derechmi*, which makes morphological sense since this land resembles Greece and the money sounds like Greek *drachma*. (*Small Gods*)

4 Hersheban coins include *dongs* and half-*dongs*. (*Jingo*)

5 Klatchian *wols* are a significant item of criminal evidence in *Jingo*.

6 The Lancre unit of currency is the Lancre penny. (*The Discworld Companion*)

7 Omnia mainly uses *obols*. (*Small Gods*)

8 Uberwald's currency is the Kram. (*Unseen University Diary 1998*)

9 XXXX is where the units of cash are squids. (*The Last Continent*)

10 The Zchloty leaden quarter *iotum*, says *The Discworld Companion*, is Discworld's smallest-denomination coin.

Bonus question: Can you deduce the currency unit of Brindisi, land of squid and pasta? (See Extra Answers, page 201.)

Vitoller's Men

Questions on page 27

1 The Dysk – named in distant memory of the Roundworld theatre for which Shakespeare wrote, the Globe. **Bonus question:** what is the rival Ankh-Morpork theatre with an animal in its name? (See Extra Answers, page 202.)

2 The play of *Wyrd Sisters*, adapted by Stephen 'Him Again' Briggs and published as *Wyrd Sisters: the play* (1996). Cramming a novel into play form requires heavy cutting, and Death's bit part ('Cower, brief mortals . . .') just didn't fit.

3 Kring claimed he wanted to be a ploughshare.

4 Fred Astaire's first screen test at RKO got the famous response from a studio executive, 'Can't act. Can't sing. Can dance a little.'

5 *Lords and Ladies*, with Comic Artisans or Rude Mechanicals played by the Lancre Morris Men.

6 As Nanny Ogg proudly said in *Maskerade*, 'our Shawn can fart any melody you care to name.' Le Pétomane (Joseph Pujol, 1857–1945) became a stage sensation by doing just this at the Moulin Rouge in the 1890s, and for a while was the highest-paid entertainer in the world.

7 Jean-Paul Sartre in his play *Huis-clos*, also known in English translation as *In Camera* or (in the USA) *No Exit*.

8 Lord Wynkin's Men, mentioned in *Lords and Ladies*.

9 The Noh play performed at the inn in *Interesting Times*. With a superhuman effort, Mr Pratchett restrained himself from describing the Aurient as 'all wok and Noh play'.

10 'Magerat, Ane Sirene.' Propaganda plays have their own strange spin on mere facts. (*Wyrd Sisters*)

Embalmers' Guild

Questions on page 28

1 *Pyramids*. It is important not to visualize this scene.

2 He kept his clock five minutes fast. A dreadful concept to the pure in heart, or at least to Jeremy. (*Thief of Time*)

3 Jeremy Bentham the philosopher (1748–1832), who on his own instructions was dissected in the presence of his friends, reconstructed with a wax replacement head, dressed in his own clothes, and placed upright in a glass case at University College, London. Stranger than Discworld. . . .

4 Big Fido, Chief Barker of the Dog Guild, in *Men at Arms*.

5 Elephants, as you might expect. **Bonus question:** what's the real-world SF resonance of this line? (See Extra Answers, page 202.)

6 Life, as it turned out, but athlete's foot was what he had in mind. (*The Truth*)

7 El-Ysa, a village in Klatch, was killed by poisoning its well. Retribution followed. (*Jingo*)

8 He had just been sucked completely dry of blood by a carriage party of vampires, which tends to explain why his next encounter was with Death. (*Carpe Jugulum*)

9 Old Vincent of the Silver Horde, in *The Last Hero*. Actually he choked on a cucumber. It's an easy mistake to make.

10 A pineapple. However improbably. (*The Last Continent*)

Country Landowners' Association

Questions on page 30

1 Nanny Ogg's phrasing of the Muntab question in *Carpe Jugulum* is considered definitive: 'Where the hell's Muntab?' William de Worde's condensed version in *The Truth* – 'Where's Muntab? – is equally acceptable as an answer.

2 Hersheba. (*Soul Music*)

3 As shown on official Mappes, it's the Contract Bridge. (*The Streets of Ankh-Morpork*)

4 Ur, as Sgt Colon discovers in *Jingo*.

5 XXXX or Fourecks, the Last Continent. (*Thief of Time*)

6 The floating, and sinking, land of Leshp whose appearance and disputed ownership triggers war between Ankh-Morpork and Klatch in *Jingo*. **Bonus question:** which classic fantasy series briefly spoofed in *The Colour of Magic* features the Sinking Land? (See Extra Answers, page 202.)

7 Transylvania, long since absorbed into Hungary, was the home of vampire legends as novelized in *Dracula*. Its name means 'across the woods' and Uberwald – home of Discworld's vampires and werewolves – is more or less German for 'over the wood'. (*Carpe Jugulum*, *The Fifth Elephant*)

8 Llamedos, the Discworld analogue of Wales. (See *The Last Hero*.)

9 Klatch, where Shelley's 'Two vast and trunkless legs of stone' in the desert waste are echoed by the huge feet and ankles which are all that remain of General Tacticus's statue. (*Jingo*)

10 The Agatean Empire, as in *Interesting Times* and *The Last Hero*.

11 Teeth – the place where Death cannot go is the secret heart of the Tooth Fairy operation. (*Hogfather*)

12 Rain. Llamedos has rain mines. (*Soul Music*)

Guild of Alchemists

Questions on page 31

1 Smash a jar of acid inside the mixture, according to Archchancellor Ridcully; the technical term for what follows is 'kablooie'. (*The Last Hero*)

2 Octo-cellulose. (*Moving Pictures*)

3 In the mining industries: 'For when they need to move mountains out of the way.' (*Jingo*)

4 Uselessium. Half a point for naming any of the alternative suggestions made by Silverfish's colleague Peavie: Ankhmorporkery, Silverfishium or Notleadium. (*Moving Pictures*)

5 *Blown Away* – much punchier, of course, than *Gone With the Wind*. (*Moving Pictures*)

6 In the Agatean Empire: it's a simple cannon, ornately shaped from metal to look like a large, fat dog with its mouth open. Half a point for pedantry if your answer was 'in Unseen University', since a Barking Dog is indeed magically transported there – and later, back again. (*Interesting Times*)

7 Billiard or snooker balls. The Alchemists should be using celluloid rather than nitrocellulose, an explosive also known as gun-cotton. (*Men at Arms*)

8 The fire at Goodmountain's printing shed, At the Sign of the Bucket, Gleam Street, off Treacle Mine Road, Ankh-Morpork. (*The Truth*) **Bonus question:** on what occasion did somone ignite a bonfire so spectacularly that the blue-white flame formed figures and castles and scenes from famous battles? (See Extra Answers, page 202.)

9 He was assisted by five thousand firecrackers – stuffed into a cauldron and left on a slow fuse by resourceful Mr

Saveloy, to distract the Forbidden City guards. (*Interesting Times*)

10 'They can gen'rally turn a house into a hole in the ground,' as Sergeant Colon put it in *The Truth* – any rough paraphrase of this insight earns a mark.

Assassins' Guild

Questions on page 32

1 The Jennings novels by Anthony Buckeridge, set at Linbury Court Preparatory School.

2 Mr Teatime in *Hogfather*. Be sure to pronounce it 'Teh-ah-tim-eh' or he might get *really* mad.

3 The gonne (gun) in *Men at Arms*. As the Patrician thought to himself, 'Some things are so perfect of their type that they are hard to destroy. One of a kind is always special.' **Bonus question:** in this case he wasn't thinking of the gonne. What had he in mind? (See Extra Answers, page 202.)

4 Foul Ole Ron, whose extraordinary Smell would keep fastidious Assassins at bay even if one were 'sufficiently mindless of his personal reputation to take this job'.

5 Dr Cruces, chief of the guild, in *Men at Arms*.

6 Inigo Skimmer, clerk to Vimes's diplomatic mission in *The Fifth Elephant*.

7 These were components of the Exploding Bustle (banned from use in most civilized countries): a lady assassin can make a discreet exit while leaving the lethal part of her costume, as it were, behind. (*Assassins' Guild Yearbook and Diary 2000*)

8 The upas tree (Sapu backwards) of Java, which according to a traveller's tale from 1783 is fatally poisonous to everything for miles around, even the grass. This was a bit of an exaggeration: the tree (*Antiaris toxicaria*) does have poisonous sap but caused no other problems when grown in Kew Gardens. (*The Last Continent*)

9 71-Hour Ahmed, in *Jingo*.

10 Jonathan, according to *Hogfather*. Or Noel, according to the *Assassins' Guild Yearbook and Diary 2000*. Have a mark for either.

Guild of Haberdashers

Questions on page 33

1 Nanny Ogg's extra-special witch's hat in *Witches Abroad*.

2 Mrs Cake's tremendous handbag in *Reaper Man*.

3 The legendary Archchancellor's Hat which by the time of *Sourcery* had soaked up magic from 2,000 years of being worn by Discworld's greatest wizards. **Bonus question:** what are Ankhstones? (See Extra Answers, page 202.)

4 The demon Astfgl's gloves in *Eric*.

5 Archchancellor Mustrum Ridcully's wizarding hat as described in *Reaper Man*.

6 A little handbag or reticule on a string, part of Granny Weatherwax's expensive Patron of the Opera outfit in *Maskerade*.

7 The utility belt worn by Teppic the trainee Assassin in *Pyramids*.

8 The protective gloves donned by the Librarian before consulting that dangerous grimoire the *Necrotelecomnicon* in *Moving Pictures*.

9 Nanny Ogg's knickers in *Maskerade*, where she stowed her royalties for *The Joye of Snacks*.

10 Concealing scarves wrapped around the necks of vampire fodder, like tight bandages, in *Carpe Jugulum*.

Guild of Apothecaries

Questions on page 34

1 Ivory, according to Mr Tulip in *The Truth*.

2 Sulphur, saltpetre and charcoal – the formula for ordinary black gunpowder, although the exact proportions are crucial. Used by Leonard's prototype rifle or 'gonne'. (*Men at Arms*)

3 Bloat – distilled from organs of the deep-sea blowfish which can inflate itself to many times normal size – causes every cell of the human body to attempt to swell up by a factor of 2,000. 'You don't need to bury the victims, just redecorate over the top.' (*Pyramids*, *The Discworld Companion*)

4 Trolls and especially troll children: this mixture is Slab, the drug that gives other races' heads an intriguing tingle but melts troll brains. (*Feet of Clay*)

5 Wow-Wow Sauce, introduced in *Reaper Man* as the favourite condiment of Archchancellor Ridcully. Apt to explode without warning.

6 The phoenix in *Carpe Jugulum*. Hodgesaargh the falconer speculated that it might need to eat inflammable materials as well as the usual bait.

7 Detritus the troll in *Men at Arms*. It's a minerally, trollish sort of drink. **Bonus question:** what's the hidden joke in that list of ingredients? (See Extra Answers, page 203.)

8 Bloody Stupid Johnson, as noted in *The Last Hero*.

9 The building of *proper* worlds, like Discworld, seemed quite impossible without these necessary elements. (*The Science of Discworld*)

10 'Salty-tasting beery brown gunk,' Rincewind's inspired creation in *The Last Continent* – recognized by Australians as Vegemite, their mysterious local allotrope of Britain's Marmite.

Guild of Actors and Mummers II

Questions on page 35

1 The Blue Bird of Happiness, unconvincing companion of the Cheerful Fairy in *Hogfather*.

2 The Librarian, during one of his involuntary morphic changes while unwell in *The Last Continent*. **Bonus question:** what was the title of the book which he later became, whose every page was covered with 'ook'? 'Good dialogue, but the plot is a little dull.' (See Extra Answers, page 203.)

3 Gaspode the Wonder Dog, thoroughly if unconvincingly disguised as a poodle called Trixiebell in *The Truth*.

4 The Cable Street Particulars (shades of the Baker Street Irregulars), the plain-clothes division of the Watch featured in *Maskerade* and *Feet of Clay*. Captain Carrot hated the idea of Watchmen in disguise.

5 The bandit chieftain who made the mistake of stopping the wizards' carriage in *Lords and Ladies*.

6 Carrot of the Watch, not quite getting the hang of plain-clothes disguise in *Jingo*.

7 Death's manservant (for want of a better word) Albert, in *Hogfather*.

8 Psychopathic Mr Tulip in *The Truth*.

9 Granny Weatherwax, playing the part of Lady Esmerelda Weatherwax in *Maskerade*.

10 Arsenic, the poison, as personified in Samuel Vimes's dream in *Feet of Clay*.

Guild of Engravers 11

Questions on page 36

1 *Jingo* – a public speaker's appeal to popular political sentiment.

2 *Feet of Clay* – Detritus's subtle anti-drug poster on the Watch House wall.

3 *Hogfather* – the label on perhaps the second most dangerous knob, tap or control of Johnson's Patent 'Typhoon' Indoor Ablutorium. **Bonus question:** which was the most dangerous? (See Extra Answers, page 203.)

4 *The Last Continent* – the escape hint left in his cell by Tinhead Ned, presumably the XXXX equivalent of Ned Kelly.

5 *Eric* – young Eric's address, supposedly scrawled on the half-title page of a book originally called *Faust*.

6 *Carpe Jugulum* – Granny Weatherwax's welcoming sign in her cavern retreat.

7 *Feet of Clay* – the written philosophy of Dorfl the golem.

8 *The Last Hero* – one of several placards of instructions transmitted by omniscope to that unique vessel the *Kite*.

9 *Maskerade*, though only hypothetically – the sign Agnes Nitt felt there ought to be on the Opera House door.

10 *Hogfather* – the notice placed on the Archchancellor's secret bathroom door, several hundred pages after defying its previous sign 'Do not, under any circumstances, open this door.' What goes around, comes around.

Mrs Widgery's Lodgers

Questions on page 37

1 A patch of temporal discontinuity. 'You had to cough before you went in, in case you were already there,' explained the Senior Wrangler in *The Last Continent*.

2 Eskarina (Esk), the girl with an illicit magical inheritance in *Equal Rites*.

3 The alley behind Unseen University where 'secretly' removable bricks have for centuries allowed students and faculty to climb over the wall. (*Jingo*)

4 It was in the squash court of the University of Chicago (at 3:45 pm on 2 December 1942) that the first human-built nuclear reactor was tested by Enrico Fermi's team of scientists, and produced a successful chain reaction. The nuclear age had begun.

5 Naturally enough, they ate the previous expedition's boots too. (*The Last Continent*)

6 It's located in the deepest cellars, and lined with lead. (*The Discworld Companion*)

7 Twenty-four hours of lying in state in the University chapel before a newly deceased wizard was actually put in the coffin. (*Reaper Man*)

8 Ridcully: 'I mean, it's not even as if it's got a keyhole on the inside . . .' (*Jingo*) **Bonus question:** what Bursarial hallucination provoked the *Ankh-Morpork Inquirer* headline HALF MAN HALF MOTH? (See Extra Answers, page 203.)

9 The correct answer is that no one knows why. Nor why a small currant bun and a copper penny should be placed on a high stone shelf there every second Wednesday. (*Hogfather*)

10 The tower of the *other* Unseen University, in Bugarup on XXXX. 'We're a clever country –' (*The Last Continent*)

Guild of Seamstresses

Questions on page 39

1 Mrs Rosie Palm herself. As noted in *The Unseen University Challenge*, the old Roundworld saying about enjoying oneself with Mrs Palm and her five lovely daughters actually indicates that the lovelorn speaker could find no female company and, as it were, took matters into his own hands.

2 Carrot in *Guards! Guards!* – when he was very new to the city.

3 Flint-knapping, according to *The Discworld Companion*. This has caused some embarrassment to knappers in quarries everywhere.

4 Angua in *Men at Arms*. Carrot, innocently: 'And you're not very good at sewing?'

5 Agnes Nitt in *Maskerade*, alias Perdita X. Nitt when seeking a musical career.

6 The Agony Aunts (Dotsie and Sadie), first mentioned in 1997 in both *The Discworld Companion* (new edition) and *Jingo*.

7 *The Perfumed Allotment, or, The Garden of Delights* (in *Jingo*) suggesting our world's exotic sex manual *The Perfumed Garden of the Sheikh Nefzaoui*. **Bonus question:** which impressionable Ankh-Morpork male bought a copy by mistake? (See Extra Answers, page 203.)

8 *Martial Arts*. King Verence: 'But I'm sure I wrote Marit –' (*Lords and Ladies*)

9 Eric the would-be demonologist, in *Eric*. When you're nearly fourteen you get ideas like this.

10 The Patrician, Lord Havelock Vetinari; the famous Roundworld study of sex was by Havelock Ellis (1859–1939).

The Librarians of
Time and Space II

Questions on page 40

1 *Feet of Clay*. Easy if you know the book: the phrase is used in the text, and the golems of the story are powered by literal magic words written on slips of paper in their ceramic heads.

2 *Hogfather*. **Bonus question:** what was the question asked by the dedicatee? (See Extra Answers, page 203.)

3 Mr Ronald Saveloy in *Interesting Times*.

4 *The Science of Discworld* by Terry Pratchett, Jack Cohen and Ian Stewart. Also, now, *The Science of Discworld* II.

5 *Terry Pratchett: Guilty of Literature* ed. Andrew M. Butler, Edward James and Farah Mendlesohn, with a particularly superb introduction by . . . oh, never mind.

6 Andrew M. Butler. He says nice thing about *The Unseen University Challenge*, thus earning himself two namechecks in this answer section.

7 *The Almanac de Gothick*, echoing our world's *Almanac de Gotha*. (*The Fifth Elephant*)

8 The Musicians' Guild, as extensively featured in *Soul Music*. Having a band on the shield is surely a pune, or play on words.

9 The fiction strand of *The Science of Discworld*, featuring Rincewind and the wizards of Unseen University.

10 Those two Josh Kirby paintings not used as Discworld jackets appeared in his 1999 art book *A Cosmic Cornucopia*.

Guild of Cooks
and Chefs

Questions on page 41

1 The wizards of Unseen University, in *Hogfather*.

2 The traditional Scots dish is finnan haddock or haddie – smoked haddock. The hearty appetitites of Ankh-Morpork naturally demand a fikkun rather a finnan. (*Men at Arms* and elsewhere)

3 Merckle and Stingbat's Very Famous Brown Sauce. (*Guards! Guards!*)

4 Chefs in upmarket restaurants take the Curious Squid and prepare, expensively and with enormous care, dishes which contain absolutely no trace of it. (*Jingo*)

5 Meat – of which the sausages in Bonk, Uberwald, are disconcertingly full. 'Where's the texture? Where's the white bits and the yellow bits and those green bits you always hope are herbs?' (*The Fifth Elephant*)

6 Nanny Ogg, who with malice aforethought served this to a select party at the Opera House in *Maskerade*.

7 The Scone of Stone in *The Fifth Elephant*. **Bonus question:** where is the similar-sounding and also politically important Roundworld object kept? (See Extra Answers, page 204.)

8 Igor in *The Truth* – that is, the particular representative of the Igor clan who joined the Ankh-Morpork City Watch in *The Fifth Elephant*.

9 In Genua, the sort of New-Orleansy city featured in *Witches Abroad*.

10 Rincewind the wizzard, after magically acquiring the powers of a bush tucker finder in *The Last Continent*.

11 Rat Surprise, in which (like the fish-heads in star-gazey pie) 'you've got to have the noses poking through the pastry'. (*Feet of Clay*)

12 Death, temporarily working as cook at Harga's House of Ribs in *Mort*.

Guild of Engravers III

Questions on page 43

1 Archchancellor Ridcully, in *The Last Continent*. 'Ridcully was to management what King Herod was to the Bethlehem Playgroup Association.'

2 *The Summoning of Dragons* by Tubal de Malachite, whose purpose is self-explanatory. (*Guards! Guards!*)

3 *Grim Fairy Tales* – more than one copy of which features in *Thief of Time*.

4 The Church of Om, once notorious for burning witches. The Roundworld *Malleus Maleficarum* is a 15th century manual of witch-hunting; the Omnian version was supposedly written by their Prophet Ossory, though with assistance. See *Carpe Jugulum*.

5 *What I Did On My Holidays*, Twoflower's account of his trip to Ankh-Morpork and environs. (*Interesting Times*)

6 A lizard press: 'You can't glue them in while they're still fat,' as the young lizard-collector who wants all these gifts (plus a display cabinet and a killing jar) explains in *Hogfather*.

7 *Practical Boat-building for Beginners* – in *The Last Continent*. **Bonus question:** which Roundworld resonance caused the Chair to ask the Dean what kind of music, under these circumstances, he'd like to listen to? (See Extra Answers, page 204.)

8 The *Guide to Impossible Buildings* is cited in the booklet of *Death's Domain: A Discworld Mapp*.

9 This and other alarmingly stimulating recipes are collected in Nanny Ogg's *The Joye of Snacks*. (*Maskerade*)

10 The Chinese general Sun Tzu's *The Art of War*, written in the early 4th century BC – our world's earliest known treatise on war and military science. (*Interesting Times*)

Minor Guilds and Societies 11

Questions on page 44

1 Their city's first printed newspaper, the *Ankh-Morpork Times* as launched in *The Truth*. **Bonus question:** of what first, tentative title was this a misprint? (See Extra Answers, page 204.)

2 It's the Guild of Plumbers and Dunnikindivers. We draw a carbolic-soaked veil over the latter's doings.

3 Who but the Guild of Accountants? (*Jingo*)

4 The Guild of Confectioners, in *Thief of Time*.

5 The Guild of Architects, in *The Truth*.

6 The Guild of C.M.O.T. Dibbler, with a membership of one. (*The Discworld Companion*)

7 The Guild of Conjurers – that is, stage magicians as opposed to wizards. The Amazing Bonko and Doris are briefly mentioned in *Equal Rites*.

8 The Guild of Glassblowers – a *real* alchemical laboratory should be filled with glassware apparently produced during their All-Comers Hiccuping Contest.

9 The Bakers' Guild – one of those heraldic puns, since Potts worked with flour (flower), fire and water. (*Feet of Clay*)

10 *The Discworld Thieves' Guild Yearbook and Diary 2002.*

The Venerable
Council of Seers

Questions on page 45

1 Presumably Young Men's Pagan Association, which as suggested in *Hogfather* is easier to say (even in initials) than Young-Men's-Reformed-Cultists-of-the-Ichor-God-Bel-Shamharoth-Association.

2 Miles and Miles of Bloody Uberwald – the great dull areas in the maps of that very large country. (*The Fifth Elephant*)

3 Leonard of Quirm's encyrption device, the multi-wheeled Engine for the Neutralizing of Information by the Generation of Miasmic Alphabets. **Bonus question:** which regime in our world used the machine to which this refers? (See Extra Answers, page 204.)

4 Burnt Crunchy Bits, a notorious contaminant in fat deposits. 'Mostly unbelievably huge and ancient animals, deep fried.' (*The Fifth Elephant*)

5 Sevrian Thomas Ungulant, full name of the hermit whom we first met as St Ungulant in *Small Gods* but who explains that his 'sainthood' was just an accident of his first two initials. This is also how the more notorious adventurer Simon Templar got his nickname, the Saint.

6 Great Big Lever, one of the controls of Unseen University's famous computer Hex. (*Hogfather*)

7 'What You Get Is What You're Given And It's No Good Whining.' (*The Science of Discworld*)

8 Special Ape Services, a hasty justification of the Librarian's presence in the Watch in *Guards! Guards!* Obviously part of a special team of crack troops called in for sieges and rescues.

9 The Phoenix, looked up by Hodgesaargh in *Carpe Jugulum*.

10 Bloody Stupid Johnson (real name Bergholt Stuttley Johnson), architect, landscape gardener, organ designer and
various other trades, whose ambitious achievements vary
wildly between genius, ineptitude, incompetence, insanity,
and total bloody stupidity.

Campaign for
Equal Heights

Questions on page 46

1 '. . . you are Dead.'

2 Nanny Ogg's red boots, in *Witches Abroad*. This is all thanks to morphic resonance with *The Wizard of Oz* – the classic movie, not L. Frank Baum's book.

3 Ankh-Morpork, with a dwarf population of 50,000 by the time of *The Fifth Elephant*.

4 Three horrible little dwarfs. These may possibly have been figments of Mrs Cosmopilite's excitable mind. (*Moving Pictures*)

5 Casanunda in *Lords and Ladies*. 'The middle of the road' may or may not be a euphemism.

6 The owner (born Thomas Smith) wasn't a dwarf but had changed his name by deed poll to Stronginthearm because people thought 'dwarf-made' must be better. (*Feet of Clay*)

7 Almost certainly Gimli, the lead dwarf character in J.R.R. Tolkien's *The Lord of the Rings*. **Bonus question:** what related cult book from the pre-Discworld era actually features a dwarf called Gimlet? (See Extra Answers, page 204.)

8 Modo is gardener at Unseen University, and looks after its lawns and grounds. (*Reaper Man* etc.)

9 Cuddy in *Men at Arms*. He's a troll-hating dwarf. His partner's a dwarf-hating troll (Detritus). They're cops. . . .

10 The Lancre Witch Trials, in 'The Sea and Little Fishes'.

11 A short. (*Men at Arms*)

12 Wee Mad Arthur the gnome, in *Feet of Clay*. The encounter was nasty for the enforcers. (The Campaign for Equal Heights tries to represent pixies and gnomes as well as dwarfs, as revealed in *Hogfather*.)

The Librarians of Time
and Space III

Questions on page 47

1 Dr Samuel Johnson of dictionary fame once said, 'When a man is tired of London, he is tired of life.'

2 The Bodleian Library in Oxford. Unlike Unseen U, the 'Bod' doesn't forbid users to explode, levitate above 2', or spontaneously combust. (*Unseen University Diary 1998*)

3 Qu of the History Monks in *Thief of Time*. Inventor of useful monkish gadgets like begging bowls that extrude hidden knife blades and then explode, Qu is a homage to the James Bond movies' master gadgeteer Q.

4 Leonard of Quirm in *Men at Arms*. His cartoons are admired by the Patrician himself, who comments: 'This is a good one of the little boy with his kite stuck in a tree.' (A recurring problem for Charlie Brown of *Peanuts*.)

5 Clement Clarke Moore – "Twas the night before Christmas . . .'

6 Elisabeth (or Erszebet) de Báthory (1560–1614) of Transylvania is recorded as having bathed in the blood of over 600 virgins in hope of preserving her youthful beauty. But not all at the same time. **Bonus question:** who does even 200 at a time seem unlikely, according to Vlad in *Carpe Jugulum*? (See Extra Answers, page 204.)

7 The classic 1870s vampire story (with a hint of lesbianism) 'Carmilla' is by J. Sheridan Le Fanu.

8 In Joseph Heller's famous war novel *Catch-22*, the rule is although anyone flying dangerous air missions must be insane, asking to be grounded because of insanity is proof of sanity. That's the catch, Catch-22. 'It's the best there is.'

9 Alfred, Lord Tennyson, who wrote these lines in his poem *Sir Galahad*.

10 In the booklet of *A Tourist Guide to Lancre: A Discworld Mapp* (1998).

Guild of Cunning
Artificers

Questions on page 49

1 The Lancre Army Knife, as specified by King Verence and constructed by Shawn Ogg in *Carpe Jugulum*.

2 Procrastinators. As the proverb goes, 'Procrastination is the thief of time.'

3 The Quizzing Device, a pub entertainment machine in *Soul Music*. Carrot cunningly substituted questions like: 'Were you nere Vortin's Diamond Warehouse on the Nite of the 15th?'

4 Peeling the potatoes in the Unseen University kitchens, in *Hogfather*.

5 The Dis-organizer that was the bane of Vimes's life in *Jingo*. Powered by a demon, this diabolically inept timekeeper was clearly a pocket organizer from Dis itself (the legendary city of Hell, as recorded in Dante's *Inferno* and elsewhere).

6 Leonard's Very-Fast-Coffee machine in *The Fifth Elephant*, producing the Discworld version of espresso coffee.

7 The mechanical malignity detector devised and operated by the Death of Rats in *Thief of Time*.

8 A concealable one-shot crossbow or spring-gonne, as carried by the Assassin in *The Fifth Elephant* and Mr Pin in *The Truth*.

9 Leonard of Quirm, who like our own world's Leonardo da Vinci writes backward, mirror-fashion. (*The Last Hero*)

10 The Graphical Device, used by schoolboy wizards to automate the writing of lines in detention class at Unseen University when the Bursar was but a lad. (*The Last Continent*)

11 The Going-Under-The-Water-Safely Device – Leonard's genius not being for names. Half a mark for his alternative suggestion 'the Boat', which echoes the classic submarine movie *Das Boot*. (*Jingo*)

12 The lavatory, named for Sir Charles Lavatory of C.H. Lavatory and Son, Mollymog Street, Ankh-Morpork. (*Soul Music*) **Bonus question:** what's the Roundworld joke here? (See Extra Answers, page 205.)

Guild of Shoemakers
and Leatherworkers

Questions on page 51

1 The primitive flip-flops or Ur-footwear devised by Rince-wind when lost in the Fourecks desert of *The Last Continent*.

2 Black button boots, according to Nanny Ogg in *Witches Abroad*.

3 Lady Sybil Ramkin's slippers, accidentally and innocently (we must stress) donned by the hurried Captain Vimes in *Guards! Guards!*

4 Unseen University's prototype Seven League Boots in *Interesting Times* – the problem being inherent in footwear that tried to make you take steps twenty-one miles long.

5 Reg Shoe the zombie, as noted in *Jingo*.

6 Ballet shoes at the Ankh-Morpork Opera House in *Masker-ade*. The music director suggested, perhaps not very sincerely, that the ballerinas could save wear on shoes by spending more time in the air . . .

7 The 'glass' shoes worn by Magrat Garlick to the Genua ball in *Witches Abroad*.

8 The kind of boots Sam Vimes of the Watch bought in his days of poverty, as recorded in *Men at Arms*. **Bonus question:** how did the contrast with good, fifty-dollar boots lead to the Vimes 'Boots' Theory of Socio-Economic Unfairness? (See Extra Answers, page 205.)

9 Several of the Unseen University wizards' shoes in *Soul Music*.

10 The boots worn by Granny Weatherwax to the Genua ball in *Witches Abroad* – same as she wore everywhere else.

11 Mr Scrope's old-established shop in Wixon's Alley, Ankh-Morpork, specializing (apparently) in erotic appliances

which are classed as leatherwork for various reasons. One was pointed out by Sam Vimes in *The Truth*: 'I don't think there's a Guild of Makers of Little Jiggly Things, although it's an interesting thought.'

12 The colossal multiple impacts as Jupiter was bombarded in 1994 by fragments of the comet Shoemaker-Levy (sorry) – as alluded to in *The Last Continent*.

Priests', Sacerdotes' and Occult Intermediaries' Guild

Questions on page 52

1 Hughnon Ridcully, chief priest of Blind Io and – as senior priest of the senior Discworld god – the nearest thing in Ankh-Morpork to a spokesman on religious affairs. (*Reaper Man*, *Feet of Clay*, etc.)

2 Om of Omnia, while inadvertently manifesting as a tortoise through most of *Small Gods*.

3 Bilious, the oh god of hangovers, in *Hogfather*. Just another characteristic symptom.

4 The Quite Reverend Mightily Oats in *Carpe Jugulum*, in order to save Granny Weatherwax from death by exposure in the wet forest.

5 A ceramic atheist: Dorfl the golem in *Feet of Clay*, who when blasted with lightning merely remarks, 'I Don't Call That Much Of An Argument.'

6 Nugganites in *The Last Hero* are forbidden to eat chocolate, ginger, mushrooms or garlic. We would not presume to enquire whether these are Pratchettian favourites, but it's permissible to wonder.

7 The God of Evolution in *The Last Continent*. Haldane is supposed to have said that if there is a God, he has an inordinate fondness for beetles – since there are about a third of a million different beetle species. (See also *The Science of Discworld*.)

8 The Hogfather underwent the Heimlich manoeuvre – violently forcing air from the lungs to dislodge a throat blockage – at the hands of Susan Sto Helit. (*Hogfather*)
Bonus question: what semi-mythic object from Twelfth

Night folklore was he choking on? (See Extra Answers, page 205.)

9 'Council of Churches, Temples, Sacred Groves and Big Ominous Rocks.' (*Feet of Clay*)

10 Inevitably, this is the cat-headed god Bast. (*Pyramids*, *The Last Hero*)

Guild of Tailors

Questions on page 53

1 Death getting into the operatic spirit of things when doing his final duty in *Maskerade*. The title character in various media versions of the *Phantom of the Opera* famously gatecrashes a party in this costume based on – **bonus question** – which classic horror story? (See Extra Answers, page 205.)

2 Otto the vampire photographer – sorry, iconographer – in *The Truth*, pockets stuffed with the mysterious paraphernalia of his art.

3 Buddy (alias Imp y Celyn) and Cliff the troll in *Soul Music*. The quotation is the most obvious of this book's several references to *The Blues Brothers*.

4 Casanunda the dwarf as seen in *Lords and Ladies*. ('Finest Swordsman, Outrageous Liar, Soldier of Fortune, Stepladders repaired.')

5 The Dean of Unseen University in *Soul Music*.

6 Miss Flitworth of *Reaper Man* must have read – or sensed morphic resonances from – Charles Dickens's *Great Expectations*. Miss Havisham in this novel acts as described, dressing as a bride even in old age after being deserted long ago on her wedding-day.

7 The wizards of the *other* Unseen University located in Bugarup on the continent XXXX, in (of course) *The Lost Continent*.

8 The wizards of 'our' Unseen University in all their dressy glory at the Convivium in *Jingo*.

9 Corporal Nobby Nobbs, secretly mingling at an Opera House reception in *Maskerade*.

10 The very small Constable Buggy Swires in *The Fifth Elephant* used 'Big Boy' rubber protectives in this unexpected way.

Ankh-Morpork City Watch II

Questions on page 54

1 A chocolate question. All but 'chocolate' itself are ingredients commonly found in locally produced Ankh-Morpork chocolate. By the higher food standards of Borogravia and Quirm, this substance is formally classed as 'cheese' and but for its colour would be 'tile grout'. (*Thief of Time*)

2 All late City Watch men who died in the line of duty, except for cheerful zombie Reg Shoe, who died before ever joining the Watch.

3 *The Use of Pliers in Warfare* is a book by General Sir Roderick Purdeigh; the rest are weapons-oriented magazines echoing real-world examples like *Guns and Ammo* or *Soldier of Fortune*. (*The Discworld Mapp* booklet; *Jingo*)

4 Delicacies offered for supper in Uberwald in *The Fifth Elephant*, with the exception of noggo, a hypothetical new metal mentioned in *The Science of Discworld*. **Bonus question:** according to Mr Pratchett's helpful footnote, walago is a kind of pastry made from which unlikely material? (See Extra Answers, page 206.)

5 Street drugs on sale in the Ankh-Morpork of *The Truth* – except for Xeno, an Ephebian philosopher of some note who appears in *Pyramids* and *Small Gods*.

6 Former questing-hero acquaintances of Cohen and the Silver Horde, listed in *Interesting Times* and mostly dead. The exception, Thog, had merely slowed down: he had to stop fighting every ten minutes to go to the lavatory.

7 Logical operators used by the magical computer Hex, with the exception of REDO, which features in error messages. (*The Science of Discworld*)

8 A Dave question. Medium Dave actually appears in *Hogfather*; a footnote explains that his nickname arose because Big Dave, Fat Dave, and the rest had aready been taken.

. 9 An eyeball question. Quoth the Raven hankers for them all the time (*Hogfather*), Norris is the Eyeball-Eating Maniac of Quirm (*Maskerade*), Susan's class gobbles 'Eyeball Pudding' (*Soul Music*) . . . but Samuel Vimes in *Jingo* firmly refuses a proffered sheep's eyeball.

10 Rumoured contents of Granny Weatherwax's mysterious box ('pretty good going for something less than a foot across'), the exception being her will – the only one of these items actually found inside. (*Lords and Ladies*)

Guild of Haberdashers II

Questions on page 55

1 White silk stockings, as reported in *Jingo*.

2 The striking hairstyles of Darleen and Letitia, girls who are not all they seem, from Discworld's equivalent of the homeland of Dame Edna Everage in *The Last Continent*.

3 'Morpork', as in Ankh-Morpork – a piece of fascinating trivia communicated by Carrot in *The Fifth Elephant*.

4 Hodgesaargh's highly speculative puppet-glove in *Carpe Jugulum*, intended to reassure a phoenix chick by looking like its parents. **Bonus question:** of which bygone television character is this description reminiscent? (See Extra Answers, page 206.)

5 Socks or possibly a woolly vest, as Death and Albert discover in *Hogfather*. Cruel and unusual punishment, perhaps.

6 The hat of Mrs Cake the medium, in *Reaper Man*.

7 The Duck Man, that member of the Ankh-Morpork street community named for the duck on his head. His standard response to the inevitable question: 'What duck?'

8 Socks, knitted from the wool of Lancre sheep by Jason Ogg or others with strong fingers, in *Carpe Jugulum*. There's a distant echo here of the ancient lyke-wake song that begins 'This ae nighte, this ae nighte . . .' and whose obstacle course for the newly dead includes the vicious thorns of Whinny-muir (whin being another name for gorse or furze) – extremely painful for those lacking 'hosen and shoon'.

9 Rincewind's wizarding hat, going native (or rather, setting a new fashion for the natives) with corks hanging from the brim in *The Last Continent*.

10 His intestines, in the prim phrasing of Willikins the butler. Lady Sybil had undoubtedly said 'have his guts for garters.' (*Jingo*)

Guild of Gamblers

Questions on page 56

These are all stated to be million-to-one chances, which on Discworld are notorious for coming up very often indeed.

1 Scant hopes of recovering the child Esk's staff in *Equal Rites*. It was on this occasion that Granny Weatherwax definitely declared, 'Million-to-one chances crop up nine times out of ten.'

2 Attempts by the Watch to adjust the odds of success for Sergeant Colon's bowshot to exactly the prescribed million to one, in *Guards! Guards!* Difficult **bonus question** for real Discworld fanatics: what was Colon's first guess at the odds before they started adjusting them? (See Extra Answers, page 206.)

3 The unlikely circumstances needed for Rincewind to return from the Dungeon Dimensions in *Eric*, according to Death.

4 Death's slim chance of defeating his official replacement in *Reaper Man*.

5 Ella's or Emberella's assumed likelihood of getting to the Genua ball in *Witches Abroad*, after the Lancre witches have nobbled her dress, footmen, horses and coach.

6 Om's plan, while still incarnated as a tortoise, to be carried by an eagle to the climactic scene of *Small Gods*.

7 Ridcully being optimistic about avoiding certain death at the hands of elves in *Lords and Ladies*.

8 Rincewind's plan to demoralize the Agatean army with rumours about invisible vampire ghosts in *Interesting Times*.

9 Detritus the troll's unlikelihood of harpooning a fleeing Klatchian ship with his crossbow in *Jingo*.

10 Ponder Stibbons begins to devise a million-to-one-chance plan to save a mission in trouble in *The Last Hero*.

The Librarians of
Time and Space IV

Questions on page 57

1 In *The Fifth Elephant*, Vimes's flight from werewolves brings him to a house gloomy with shades of Russian drama and especially the plays of Anton Chekhov: *Uncle Vanya*, he of the gloomy trousers, and *The Three Sisters* bickering in their lonely home about whether to chop down *The Cherry Orchard* . . .

2 'The Peeled Nuts' subtly echoes the Roundworld society devoted to re-enacting the English Civil War, the Sealed Knot.

3 Scrabble, as further indicated by blue squares with a 'Three Times Ye Value Of Thee Letter' score. (*Jingo*)

4 The Moon, as indicated by the title *The Man in the Moone: or a Discourse of a Voyage Thither by Domingo Gonsales, the Speedy Messenger*, published in 1638. **Bonus question:** who was the author? (See Extra Answers, page 206.)

5 Benjamin Franklin, to someone who asked what was the use of a new invention: 'What is the use of a new-born child?'

6 Tommy Handley's 1939–49 BBC radio comedy show ITMA (*It's That Man Again*) featured the regular 'Oriental' character Ali Oop. Typical lines: 'You buy very saucy postcard. Very funny, oh lumme . . . No postcard, mister? Pity. All right. I go – I come back.'

7 *Crackerjack* (BBC), a variety show including a quiz whose young contestants had to hold on to all the prizes they won, plus a cumbersome cabbage for each wrong answer. Dropping anything meant that you dropped out.

8 Samuel Vimes's ancestor Suffer-Not-Injustice Vimes, nick-named Old Stoneface, who killed the unpleasant King

Lorenzo – last king of Ankh-Morpork. Like Cromwell, Old Stoneface had warts, and his troops were called Ironheads as a nod to Cromwell's Roundheads. (*Feet of Clay*)

9 *The Water Babies* (1863) by Charles Kingsley – whose Discworld version led Colon to believe in an undersea paradise where you could breathe. But instead: 'It's all bloody *lies* about the sea. It's just all yuk with lobsters in it.' (*Jingo*)

10 The Wallace novel is *The Door With Seven Locks*, and the Occult Sequence is the key to the seven magical locks on a door in *Hogfather*.

College of Heralds

Questions on page 59

1 Lord Snapcase, himself preceded by Lord Winder – as we learn in *Feet of Clay*.

2 Archchancellor Mustrum Ridcully in *The Science of Discworld*. **Bonus question:** Why this variety of names? (See Extra Answers, page 206.)

3 Rincewind, on entering the Unseen University of XXXX in *The Last Continent*.

4 The Cheerful Fairy in *Hogfather*. (The Senior Wrangler answered, 'Yes.')

5 Mr Thumpy, naturally. Sorry . . . the temporarily sapient rabbit of Holy Wood, encountered in *Moving Pictures*.

6 William de Worde, and also of course his father Lord de Worde, in *The Truth*.

7 The Luggage, by the Petunia (Desert Princess) collective in *The Last Continent*.

8 Bibulous, as revealed in *Hogfather*.

9 The Vimes family, thanks to one of those hilarious heraldic linkages: grapes, vines, Vimes. (*Feet of Clay*)

10 In our Roundworld, the Selachii are the shark family.

Philosophers' Tavern II

Questions on page 60

1 'The Buck Starts Here.' Seen on Ridcully's desk in *The Last Continent*, along with his *other* sign: 'When You're Up to Your Ass in Alligators, Today Is the First Day of the Rest of Your Life.'

2 'Is the High Priest an Offlian?' – that is, 'Is the Pope a Catholic?' (*Men at Arms*)

3 'The marthter does not drink . . . beer?' Vimes is of course teetotal by the time of *The Fifth Elephant*. **Bonus question:** which famous movie line, also echoed in *Carpe Jugulum*, is referred to here? (See Extra Answers, page 206.)

4 'The leopard does not change his shorts.' This seems very true. (*Carpe Jugulum*)

5 'Does a bear poo in the woods?' – Susan has spent too much time teaching small children in *Thief of Time*.

6 'Does a dragon explode in the woods?' – swamp dragons are all too notorious for this mishap, in the woods or anywhere else. (*Men at Arms*)

7 'Does a camel shit in the desert, sir?' (*Jingo*)

8 'The worm is on the other boot now', says the oh god of hangovers in *Hogfather*, subtly mingling our sayings 'The worm has turned' and 'The boot (or shoe) is on the other foot now'.

9 'A nod's as good as a poke with a sharp stick to a deaf camel,' says Dhblah in *Small Gods*.

10 'There's many a slip twixt dress and drawers.' (*Wyrd Sisters*)

Guild of Interpreters II

Questions on page 61

1 'Autocondimentor'. (*Reaper Man*)

2 *Samizdat.* Try saying it aloud. Better still, don't. (*Interesting Times*)

3 *Knobless obleeje* according to Nobby, and *Nobblyesse obligay* according to Colon, but any plausible approximation to *Noblesse oblige* scores you a point. (*Feet of Clay*)

4 'Vindaloo'. (*Jingo*)

5 *Grand Guignol.* (*Maskerade*)

6 *Photus*, on the basis that it's the root of 'photographer'. (*The Truth*)

7 Croissaint Rouge Pursuivant (Red Crescent), a dignitary of the College of Heralds. (*Feet of Clay*)

8 'Aargh!' – frequently on Rincewind's lips in *Interesting Times*. **Bonus question:** according to the Dean in the same book, what is the word for a tyrannical and repressive form of government? (See Extra Answers, page 207.)

9 FABRICATE DIEM, PVNC. (*Guards! Guards!*)

10 'Charisn'tma', the opposite of charisma. (*Feet of Clay*)

Guild of Lawyers

Questions on page 62

1 In Dunmanifestin atop the mountain Cori Celesti, the home of Discworld's gods. (*Small Gods*)

2 'Remember Never To Forget Rule One,' as recorded in *Thief of Time*. **Bonus question:** what, then, is Rule One? (See Extra Answers, page 207.)

3 Cripple Mr Onion.

4 Borrowing, as practised by Granny Weatherwax in *Lords and Ladies*.

5 Gnomes, with particular reference to Buggy Swires in *The Fifth Elephant*.

6 Roundworld Project astrophysics in *The Science of Discworld*. There, large quantities of matter somehow collect into balls rather than more natural shapes like turtles. It is a mystery.

7 If the Tooth Fairy doesn't have the exact 50p change to pay for the tooth under a child's pillow, she has to pull out another to make the fee up to a dollar – the audit rules insist that teeth and cash paid must match exactly. (*Soul Music*)

8 The Agatean Empire of *Interesting Times*.

9 Black leather. (*The Last Continent*) There can be no connection with Terry Pratchett's fondness for black leather hats.

10 The Librarians of Time and Space, as recorded in *Guards! Guards!*

Guild of Actors
and Mummers III

Questions on page 63

1 Teppic – and all the other pharaohs of Djelibeybi in their day – had to wear this gold mask as part of a dreadfully extensive set of god-kingly regalia. (*Pyramids*)

2 Greebo the cat, while temporarily in human shape, selected a ginger cat mask for the ball in *Witches Abroad*: 'Aaalwaaays waanted to bee ginger.'

3 The Opera House Phantom's mask is so described in *Maskerade*.

4 A Willie the Vampire mask, in which Ridcully would leap at the Bursar from behind doors in *Men at Arms*. This did not, surprisingly, cure his nervousness.

5 A skeleton (or skelington) mask for trick-or-treating (trickle-treating), in *Reaper Man*.

6 A cheap carnival mask: fake spectacles, big pink nose, heavy black moustache. Strange are the ways of the truly enlightened. (*Thief of Time*)

7 Walter Plinge – this being the real murderer's characterization of him without his mask in *Maskerade*.

8 At the Genua ball in *Witches Abroad*, the impressive item in question being Death's mask or lack of one.

9 *The Man in the Iron Mask*. But instead, Vetinari's double suffered the crueller fate of impersonating him at children's parties. (*The Truth*)

10 Hwel in *Witches Abroad*, momentarily resonating to the influence of the masked Phantom of the Opera before

rewriting one of the funny bits to allow for the fact that the hero had been born in a handbag. **Bonus question:** which classic but mask-free comedy does that next bit refer to? (See Extra Answers, page 207.)

Guild of Merchants
and Traders II

Questions on page 64

1 The banana – supposedly related to the Krullian pipefish, which is likewise yellow and goes around in bunches or shoals. (*Hogfather*)

2 Horseradish. (*Feet of Clay*)

3 Cabbages; the tavern in Scrote is called The Jolly Cabbage. (*Soul Music*)

4 A variety of apple. 'Tasty, a bit wrinkled, but a damn good keeper,' as Nanny remarked. ('The Sea and Little Fishes')

5 Mr Pin in *The Truth*, last seen – or is he? – in the form of a potato.

6 The apple, as in Death's cry APPLE! SAUCE! in *Hogfather*. Albert: 'It'd bloody well work on me if I was a pig . . .'

7 A tomato plant – a new breed that grew enormously at the expense of all the other vegetables which it viciously attacked. (*The Fifth Elephant*)

8 The copious multi-species dung produced by the College's zoo of heraldic animals. (*Feet of Clay*)

9 'She Sits Among the Cabbages and Leeks.' (*Maskerade*)

10 The wahooni or wahoonie. (Discworld *passim*) **Bonus question:** what, then, is known as the Great Wahoonie? (See Extra Answers, page 207.)

Cable Street Particulars

Questions on page 65

1 His grandmother's funeral, as recorded in *Feet of Clay*.

2 Clamping the Ankh-Morpork Opera House. Which, admittedly, *was* an obstacle to traffic. (*The Fifth Elephant*)

3 *Feet of Clay* mentions two magazines: *Battle Call*, echoing the Salvation Army's *War Cry*, or *Unadorned Facts*, echoing – **bonus question** – which American publication? (See Extra Answers, page 207.)

4 Pigeons. Constable Downspout, a gargoyle, lived on them and was interested in little else. This led to unfortunate incidents with Watch messenger pigeons. (*Feet of Clay*, *Jingo*)

5 Detritus the troll. (*Maskerade*)

6 Cheery Littlebottom the dwarf alchemist. (*Feet of Clay*)

7 Probationary Constable Buggy Swires, a gnome, appears as a Watch member in *Jingo* and may or may not be the gnome Swires from *The Light Fantastic*.

8 Constable Visit (half a mark), more properly Constable Visit-The-Infidel-With-Explanatory-Pamphlets (a full mark), introduced in *Feet of Clay* and nicknamed Washpot by his colleagues.

9 *Discworld Noir*, the fourth official Discworld computer game. All right, that's the one question about Discworld computer games. There are no more.

10 The Patrician had agreed that 'the Watch must reflect the ethnic makeup of the City'. Cosmetics were clearly involved. (*Men at Arms*)

Guild of Fools
and Joculators II

Questions on page 66

1 ' "A Watch from, your Old Freinds in the Watch", this is a pune or Play on Words,' writes Carrot in *Men at Arms*.

2 'A puffin,' according to the Bursar in *The Last Continent*.

3 'Lyre.' Nobby is unable to resist this pune in *Soul Music*.

4 *Déjà-fu*, as practised by Lu Tze in *Thief of Time*.

5 'You always been dead against zombies, excuse my pune,' says Colon in *Feet of Clay*, referring to Vimes's prejudices about suitable Watch recruits.

6 ... YOU'LL BE BJORN AGAIN. Death's attempt to cheer up a sad occasion in *Men at Arms* went down like a lead balloon, alas, with the just-deceased Bjorn. **Bonus question:** what is 'Bjorn Again' in our world? (See Extra Answers, page 207.)

7 'Can't make both ends meat, eh?' (*The Truth*)

8 '. . . a brace of sheikhs.' (*Jingo*)

9 Felonious Monk, i.e. the Roundworld jazz hero Thelonious Monk. (*Soul Music*)

10 'Even if it is a bit of a squash.' The Chair of Indefinite Studies was very proud of this pune and tried quite hard to explain it. (*The Last Continent*)

Guild of Apothecaries II

Questions on page 67

1 Nobby Nobbs, who couldn't understand why everyone gave him bath stuff as Hogswatch presents: 'I can't think why, 'cos it's not as if I hardly ever *has* a bath.' (*Hogfather*)

2 The Alchemists' Guild, as recorded in *Jingo*.

3 Granny Weatherwax in *Maskerade*.

4 Angua the werewolf, whose keen sense of smell was massively overloaded by this stink-bomb formula in *The Truth*.

5 Rats, according to Miss Flitworth in *Reaper Man*.

6 Immortality, according to alchemists; but then an alchemist would cut his own head off if he thought it would make him live longer. (*The Last Continent*)

7 Hex, the Unseen University computer, which had gone a little crazy in *Hogfather* and was given this typed-in remedy. **Bonus question:** what affliction was Hex suffering from? (See Extra Answers, page 207.)

8 Either *aqua fortis*, concentrated nitric acid, or *aqua regia*, a mixture of nitric and hydrochloric acids that can dissolve gold. A point for either answer. (*Feet of Clay*)

9 Tame lightning, or what we would call electricity. The Alchemists' Guild scoffed, but it's a workable if low-current battery. (*Men at Arms*)

10 Death. These are ingredients for streamlined versions of the Rite of AshkEnte which summons him. (Discworld *passim*)

Guild of Engravers
and Printers

Questions on page 68

1 Goodmountain, chief of the dwarf printers, has a name which is a translation (from German) of a famous early printer: Gutenberg. Like everything in this section, he features in *The Truth*.

2 De Worde is such an obvious name for someone who deals in words that it appeared in our own history too. Wynkyn de Worde, born Jan Van Wynkyn, was a 15th/16th century printer who worked at William Caxton's press (the first in Britain) and took it over when Caxton died. **Bonus question:** where did William de Worde make his first appearance in the Discworld context? (See Extra Answers, page 208.)

3 Boddonny of the dwarf printing team echoes the Round-world font or typeface known as Bodoni.

4 The non-misprinted version is Biblical: St John, chapter 8, verse 32. 'And ye shall know the truth, and the truth shall make you free.'

5 Caslong . . . as for Boddonny above, with the font Caslon.

6 Bizarrely, rats nibbling at the waxed leather pneumatic tubes were the downfall of Ireland's air-powered Kingstown (now Dun Laoghaire) to Dalkey Atmospheric Railway, which opened in March 1844 but whose profits were soon literally eaten away. Pratchett adds: 'Funny how you do a lot of research for the sheer fun of learning how complex a communication system could get without electricity, and end up with one line. . . .'

7 Gowdie . . . as for Boddonny above, with the font family Goudy (named for the US typographer who designed it).

8 Although the phrase has a hilariously crude meaning in *The Truth*, the original 'The King of the Golden River' is an 1850 fairytale for children by British writer and art critic John Ruskin.

9 'Publish and be damned' was supposedly written by the Duke of Wellington across a blackmailing letter suggesting that for a suitable fee he could be omitted from Harriette Wilson's imaginatively spicy *Memoirs* (1825). Many other notables paid to be left out of a book whose first line went: 'I shall not say why and how I became, at the age of fifteen, the mistress of the Earl of Craven.' (But 'Wellington' is a sufficient answer!)

10 Alludes to a famous and much misquoted verse, often credited to Anonymous but in fact the only surviving fragment of Humbert Wolfe's forgotten 1930 verse novel *The Uncelestial City*. A full mark if your answer included any phrase of the definitive text:

> *You cannot hope*
> *to bribe or twist,*
> *thank God! the*
> *British journalist.*
> *But, seeing what*
> *the man will do*
> *unbribed, there's*
> *no occasion to.*

Campaign for
Dead Rights

Questions on page 69

1 The bar where the undead drink is Biers, introduced in *Feet of Clay* – 'bier' for that funeral touch, sounding like 'beer' and echoing the US TV comedy series set in a bar, *Cheers*.

2 Vampire watermelons, strangely enough – one of the novel's totally bizarre and obviously Pratchett-invented superstitions which in fact exists in the real world.

3 Mrs Drull was a ghoul, but the problem with her meat patties was just that she couldn't cook very well. (*Reaper Man*)

4 Vampires. Clerks had small chance of promotion in this firm since 'dead men's shoes were being fully occupied by dead men'. (*Maskerade*)

5 Bogeymen. Everyone knows from childhood that they go away if you put your head under the blanket; putting *their* head under a blanket reduces them to moaning existential uncertainty. (*Feet of Clay*)

6 Windle Poons in *Reaper Man*, the wizards having decided that a zombie *needed* burial at a crossroads. **Bonus question:** which were the two crossing streets? (See Extra Answers, page 208.)

7 The *old* Count de Magpyr in *Carpe Jugulum*. As Igor says, 'Old Red Eyeth ith back!'

8 Reg Shoe the zombie Watchman, serving in Sir Samuel Vimes's First of Foot. He hit people with his chopped-off arm and they ran away screaming. (*Jingo*)

9 The Tooth Fairy collection scheme, in *Hogfather*.

10 This was the accident-prone vampire in *Feet of Clay*, who was staked in the pencil factory and had other mishaps stacking garlic, working in holy water manufacture, etc. . . .

Guild of Accountants II

Questions on page 70

1 Ages of the two Ankh-Morpork street gangs temporarily reformed by Carrot in *Jingo*. **Bonus question:** can you remember the names of the gangs? Not Bloods or Crips. (See Extra Answers, page 208.)

2 Camels, in *Jingo*.

3 XXXX or Fourecks, the book itself being *Dangerous Mammals, Reptiles, Amphibians, Birds, Fish, Jellyfish, Insects, Spiders, Crustaceans, Grasses, Trees, Mosses, and Lichens of Terror Incognita*. (*The Last Continent*)

4 Rat-skins, collected and sold by Wee Mad Arthur in *Feet of Clay*.

5 71-Hour Ahmed, the scarred Klatchian with the big curvy sword who causes the Watch no end of hassle in *Jingo*.

6 Samuel Vimes's City Watch badge number is 177. (*Men at Arms*)

7 The 512 Commandments (to date) in the Omnian religion at the time of *Small Gods*.

8 Bloody Stupid Johnson's ornamental fountain in the Ankh-Morpork palace grounds. (*Men at Arms*)

9 Ankh-Morpork dollar coins, as significantly weighed in *The Truth*.

10 Sherry, put out for the Hogfather and drunk by Albert in *Hogfather*.

Silicon
Anti-Defamation
League

Questions on page 71

1 A Balrog. (*Moving Pictures*) One-quarter of a mark if you answered Balrog, a major nasty from Tolkien's *The Lord of the Rings*.

2 Detritus of the Watch. The warehouse interior was icy cold, which stimulates troll brains to think faster. Superconductivity is implicated. (*Men at Arms*)

3 He claimed to be the (nonexistent) Troll Tooth Fairy. (*Feet of Clay*) **Bonus question:** what fairylike yet trollish name did he give? (See Extra Answers, page 208.)

4 Cliff, alias Lias Bluestone, the troll drummer in *Soul Music*. Either name will do.

5 Detritus again: the Piecemaker is his giant siege crossbow, adapted to fire a bundle of several dozen arrows simultaneously in *The Fifth Elephant*.

6 'A Big Troll & Some Other Trolls'. (*Soul Music*)

7 *Tons.* (*The Truth*)

8 Slab, the hard drug of the troll world. (*Feet of Clay*)

9 Cohen the Barbarian, whose dentures were made from fragment of a troll's diamond tooth. (*The Light Fantastic*, *Interesting Times*)

10 The Cavern. (*Soul Music*)

11 *Guys and Trolls* in *Maskerade*, echoing *Guys and Dolls* (which was based on a short story by Damon Runyon: see 'Thieves' Guild II', page 189).

12 The Mae West line goes: 'Is that a pistol in your pocket or are you just glad to see me?' Also quoted as 'a gun' or 'your sword' . . . any of these will do. (*Moving Pictures*)

The Sages of the
Unknown Shadow

Questions on page 72

1 Bachelor of Fluencing, an easily obtained qualification at Unseen University, whose abbreviation gives quiet amusement to the citizenry. (*The Discworld Companion* and elsewhere) **Bonus question:** what puzzling bachelor degree is the B.El.L.? (See Extra Answers, page 208)

2 Bugarup University in the city of Bugarup, XXXX. This is implied rather than definitely spelt out in *The Last Continent.*

3 Broomsticks Airborne, one of the strangely reminiscent commercial flight names (like Three Witches Airborne, or even Virgin) discussed by the wyrd sisters in *Witches Abroad.*

4 PONGO, the name on the collar worn by the orangutan Librarian when disgustedly posing as a pet in *Lords and Ladies*, is presumably short for his species classification *Pongo pygmaeus.*

5 Examples of Pigeon Code appear in *Ankh-Morpork City Watch Diary 1999.*

6 GV19 forms feature in the paperwork of the Tooth Fairy collection operation in *Hogfather* (specifically, receipts signed by the cart driver for each load of teeth, but no need to have remembered that).

7 QWB is the abbreviation used for the Quantum Weather Butterfly – noted for its fractal-patterned wings – in *The Discworld Companion.*

8 Eta Beta Pi or Eat A Better Pie is the unofficial motto of Unseen University's determinedly well-fed wizards. (*Hogfather*)

9 This is short for One-Man-Pouring-a-Bucket–of-Water-over-Two-Dogs, named for the first thing seen by his mother after the birth. His twin brother, ten seconds older, was less fortunate. (*Reaper Man*)

10 *The Unseen University Challenge* – that is, the previous Discworld quizbook. (Sorry about that.)

Strippers' Guild

Questions on page 73

1 What could she be but Miss VaVa Voom (stage name of Miss Dixie Voom)? **Bonus question:** what is her Guild role following her farewell performance? (See Extra Answers, page 208.)

2 Nobby Nobbs, when wearing drag in *Jingo*.

3 Foul Old Ron in *Men at Arms*. Angua of the Watch stripping in haste was the kind of thing he saw all the time, though usually only on the inner side of his head.

4 Trolls don't normally wear much in the way of clothes, so a troll stripper excites the audience by donning garment after garment, 'often causing a riot as the fourth overcoat goes on'. (*The Discworld Companion*)

5 A naked man, hotly pursued by members of the Watch. (*The Truth*)

6 Granny Weatherwax: '*I'm* not. I got three vests on.' (*Witches Abroad*)

7 In his bath. Credit for this dastardly deed was claimed by Boy Willie of the Silver Horde. (*Interesting Times*)

8 Bibulous, God of Wine, in *Hogfather*.

9 Archchancellor Ridcully, in *The Last Continent*.

10 Swamp dragons, often misused as paint strippers. (*Guards! Guards!*)

Guild of Armourers

Questions on page 74

1 'Money back if not completely decapitated.' (*Jingo*)

2 The double-handed axe. (*Interesting Times*) **Bonus question:** why would a strangling rope or candlestick seem a more likely choice of weapon? (See Extra Answers, page 209.)

3 Hogswatch, the equivalent of Christmas: a toy Klatchian War Chariot was the scheduled present for eight-year-old James Riddlc *if* he'd been good. . . . (*Hogfather*)

4 Sunlight, focused on the ships by a 30-foot parabolic mirror devised by the philosophers of Ephebe. (*Small Gods*) Archimedes is said to have done something similar during the defence of Syracuse in 212 BC. Some later scientists doubted this: J. B. S. Haldane reckoned that Archimedes didn't build the weapon but 'perhaps the Syracusan Ministry of Information dropped leaflets over the walls saying that he was going to'.

5 Carrot's groin protective, worn over the vitals when he first came to Ankh-Morpork. (*Guards! Guards!*)

6 Battle bread, subsequently displayed in the Dwarf Bread Museum. (*Feet of Clay*)

7 The Klatchian Fire Engine, a species of flamethrower. (*Men at Arms*)

8 Nobby Nobbs. He got one as his Hogswatch present, too. (*Hogfather*)

9 Chocolate. (*Thief of Time*)

10 Swamp dragons, as pets. (*Men at Arms*)

College of Heralds II

Questions on page 75

1 A small owl. (*Feet of Clay*) Pratchett fans had pointed out that in our own world, 'morepork' was one of two birds, the frogmouth in Australia and a small brown owl in New Zealand. The city coat of arms, an owl perched on an ankh, was thus inevitable.

2 Merry ravens. (*Hogfather*)

3 The time of day; for example, at three o'clock in the afternoon the beetle turns a somersault. (*Thief of Time*)

4 'Some of the sheep.' (*The Last Continent*)

5 The Eater of Socks, as accidentally brought into existence at Unseen University to the detriment of the wizards' laundry. (*Hogfather*)

6 The weather in the near future, according to a footnote in *Hogfather*. **Bonus question:** which Roundworld creature does the 'Burglar Crab' most resemble? (See Extra Answers, page 209.)

7 The painting is *Woman Holding Ferret*. (*The Truth, Thief of Time*)

8 Death's domain, where the black peacocks' tails are patterned with skulls. (*Death's Domain: A Discworld Mapp*)

9 A buzzard trained, or partly trained, by Lancre falconer Hodgesaargh. (*Carpe Jugulum*)

10 The yudasgoat, or Judas goat. (*Feet of Clay*)

Guild of Architects

Questions on page 76

1 The Hogfather. (*Hogfather*)

2 The university's New Tower, magically erected by Coin the sourcerer but short-lived. (*Sourcery*)

3 The Unreal Estate. (*The Truth*)

4 The Dwarf Bread Museum. (*Feet of Clay*)

5 His Shed of Doom. (*The Last Hero*)

6 The Opera House – see especially *The Streets of Ankh-Morpork.*

7 The Library of Ephebe, in *Small Gods.*

8 The Tanty is the Ankh-Morpork city jail. (*The Discworld Companion* and later books.)

9 The Seriph of Al-Khali in *Sourcery*. The typically Pratchettian linkage goes: oriental palace . . . the Alhambra in Granada . . . common name for cinemas of yore . . . Roxy another such name . . . Rhoxie. **Bonus question:** the Rhoxie having legendarily been built in a single night by a genie, what was its other nickname? (See Extra Answers, page 209.)

10 The triumphal arch lived in a small cardboard box (which is a sufficient answer), normally in the pocket of the Official Keeper of the Monuments. Another trifling error in architectural scale by Bloody Stupid Johnson. (*Men at Arms*)

Guild of Musicians II

Questions on page 77

1 'A Wizard's Staff Has a Knob on the End' – one of Discworld's enduring, and probably rowdy, popular songs. (*Wyrd Sisters* and others)

2 Rogers and Hammerstein (Hammerjug), responsible for many musical outbreaks including *The Sound of Music*. (*Soul Music*)

3 Bugarup, in XXXX – reflecting Australian pride in the Sydney Opera House. (*The Last Continent*)

4 Hens are not noted for greeting the dawn. Cocks are, but Mrs Huggs had a nervously prudish way with traditional wordings. (*Hogfather*)

5 Mr Clete had been in the Fools' Guild; half a mark for naming his even more previous employers, the Thieves. (*Soul Music*)

6 The dwarfs of Uberwald, as recounted in *The Fifth Elephant*. **Bonus question:** who in this novel sang Ironhammer's 'Ransom' song to tremendous effect? (See Extra Answers, page 209.)

7 '. . . So good they named it Ankh-Morpork!' (*Reaper Man*)

8 It translates as 'Johnny Be Good' – hence Chuck Berry's very famous 'Johnny B. Goode'. (*Soul Music*)

9 The Hiho Song, whose known lyrics consist of: 'Hihohiho. Hihohiho.' (*Moving Pictures*)

10 Christine, the opera singer who couldn't actually sing too well, in *Maskerade*.

Smugglers' Guild

Questions on page 78

1 *Hogfather* – where a version of the mindlessly chatty ELIZA computer program runs on Hex at Unseen University, parrying the Bursar's babblings with '+++ Tell Me About Your Spoon +++' and '+++ How Long Have You Been Mr Jelly? +++'

2 *The Last Continent* – similarly featuring Aussie drag queens travelling the country in their reminiscently named cart 'Petunia, the Desert Princess'.

3 *The Last Hero* – where it turns out that the gods leave maps and other stuff around to lure heroes to their deaths.

4 *Hogfather* – *A Christmas Carol* notoriously ends with Tiny Tim's line 'God Bless Us, Every One!', echoed (without the capitals) by Arnold Sideways in the last scene of *Hogfather*.

5 *Guards! Guards!* – in which the small dragon Errol, referred to by breeders as a no-hoper, runt or 'whittle', re-invents his own internal plumbing as a jet engine.

6 *Jingo* – although the Discworld assassination attempt has a rather different outcome, there are many parallels. These include the shot fired from the fifth floor of the Texas Schools Book Depository or of Unseen University Library respectively, the public procession, the plaza location (Dealey Plaza; the Plaza of Broken Moons), the murder of the attacker, the debate about angles of fire and a possible second marksman . . . **Bonus question:** how does Stoolie the nonhuman informer of Ankh-Morpork echo the tangle of Kennedy conspiracy theories? (See Extra Answers, page 209.)

7 *Feet of Clay* or *Jingo* – both telling how General Tacticus of Ankh-Morpork was sent to Genua when that city requested

a king. In the best interests of Genua he then proceeded to declare war on Ankh-Morpork.

8 *Hogfather* – where children's imaginations conjure up bears which like those in the Milne poem will eat you up if you step on the cracks in the pavement.

9 *Jingo* – featuring Gulli, Gulli and Beti of Klatch, whose clothes and props were appropriated by visitors from Ankh-Morpork.

10 *The Fifth Elephant* – in which Uberwaldian history includes a treaty thrashed out at the Diet of Bugs.

11 *Interesting Times* – where legend records that the Great Wizard of the Agatean Empire flew a kite that trapped the lightning in the sky.

12 *Guards! Guards!* – the LAPD motto is 'To Protect and to Serve', the alleged motto of the Watch. Half a mark for answering *Feet of Clay*, where a similar Latinized phrase (*Protego Et Servio*) features in the Vimes coat of arms.

Guild of Cunning
Artificers II

Questions on page 79

1 Ajandurah's Wand of Utter Negativity, used by Marchesa to threaten Rincewind and Twoflower in *The Colour of Magic*, had the nasty ability not only to destroy you but – retrospectively – to cause you never to have existed.

2 The Barbarian Invaders Machine was a game found in the Mended Drum tavern at the time of *Soul Music*. Basically, it was Space Invaders recreated in laborious clockwork detail, quite probably by Leonard of Quirm.

3 The Device of Erratic Balls features in devotional martial arts training among the History Monks in *Thief of Time*. It hurls random balls at you – to be caught or dodged, whichever seems wiser.

4 The Phase of the Moon Generator has something uncertain to do with computation, being part of Unseen University's occult computer Hex. (Real-world programs whose output is erratic or unreliable are often said to depend on POM, the phase of the moon.)

5 Prince Haran's Tiller is the equivalent of an autopilot, devised by Leonard of Quirm for his flying ship in *The Last Hero*.

6 The Make-Things-Bigger Device, used for military observations in *Jingo*, is evidently a telescope.

7 The Marquis of Fantailler Rules were a code of honour for 'the noble art of fisticuffs', as cited in *The Fifth Elephant* and corresponding to the Marquess of Queensberry's rules for Roundworld boxing. Totally useless against the average dirty fighter, of course.

8 The Ornamental Cruet Set of Mad Lord Snapcase, designed by the scale-challenged Bloody Stupid Johnson, was a splendid contribution to housing and storage: 'four families live in the salt shaker and we use the pepper pot for storing grain.' (*Men at Arms*)

9 Weezencake's Unreliable Algorithm is an obsolete means of reading invisible writings, according to *The Last Continent*.

10 Wheelbright's Gravity Escapement is for timekeeping – one of the clock components listed in *Thief of Time*. **Bonus question:** in the same book, Wilframe Balderton was said to have imagined the Fish Tail Escapement after eating too much what? (See Extra Answers, page 209.)

Beggars' Guild

Questions on page 80

1 The Misbegot Bridge. (*Soul Music, Feet of Clay, The Truth*)

2 Death, in *Soul Music*.

3 Arnold Sideways has no legs. But he has a useful boot on a stick all the same. (*Hogfather*)

4 Foul Ole Ron, whose personal Smell led a semi-independent life and became too striking to perceive with the mere nose, which tended to shut down in self-defence. (*Soul Music*)

5 Queen Molly of the Beggars. It would be beneath the dignity of the chief beggar to request small change. (*Men at Arms*)

6 All but Cumbling Michael are the multiple personalities of eightfold street person Altogether Andrews. (*The Truth*)

7 Wear a sack over his head. Otherwise, he gave people 'an unnerving feeling that they were upside down'. (*Jingo*)

8 Coffin Henry. (*Soul Music*)

9 Gaspode the Wonder Dog, loosely attached to Foul Ole Ron as his thinking-brain dog. (*Feet of Clay*)

10 The Bursar of Unseen University in *Lords and Ladies*, although Foul Ole Ron later made it his own. **Bonus question:** for obsessives only, where did Terry Pratchett get the phrase? (See Extra Answers, page 209.)

Ankh-Morpork
City Watch III

Questions on page 81

1 All these groups have now (2002) had their own Discworld Yearbook and Diary volumes, with the exception of the not really terribly interesting Butchers.

2 Noble families of the Agatean Empire, except Hunghung, which is a city there. (*Interesting Times*)

3 Forenames of males in the Carter family of Lancre, except (Harry) Dread, who features in *The Last Hero*.

4 Names of golems from *Feet of Clay*, except 'Knurd', a reversed spelling that describes a state of extreme and unbearable sobriety.

5 Dames of Discworld opera (see *Maskerade* and *The Last Continent*), except Sybil Ramkin, an amateur singer whose title is Lady.

6 Varieties of swamp dragon from a list in *The Last Hero*, with the exception of (Spold's) Unstirring Divisor, a wizards' spell debated in *Hogfather*. **Bonus question:** why do we suspect that 'Bridisian Courser', another dragon from that list in *The Last Hero* (first edition), may be a misprint? (See Extra Answers, page 210.)

7 Patricians of Ankh-Morpork, past and present – except Lord Rust, a mere 'ordinary' member of the nobility. (*Men at Arms*, *Jingo*)

8 Gouger, Rooter, Snouter and Tusker are the legendary pigs who pull the Hogswatchnight sleigh in *Hogfather*; the odd one out, Slasher, is a nickname of a couple of non-pig characters in other Discworld books.

9 The Four Horsemen of Panic, as listed in *Interesting Times*; and so the exception is Panic itself. Or himself.

10 Eye-watering words from the rituals of the Elucidated Brethren in *Guards! Guards!* – with the exception of tridlins, found in another context. (Nobby: 'A man could probably have his tridlins plucked just for thinking about . . .')

Fine Art Appreciation
Society

Questions on page 82

1 The *Mona Ogg*. (*Men at Arms*)

2 The ferret's nose. (*The Truth*)

3 Willow-pattern china. (*Interesting Times*)

4 Lord Vetinari in *Feet of Clay*. **Bonus question:** what well-known Roundworld political treatise of the 17th century was illustrated by a similar composite, crowned figure representing the state? (See Extra Answers, page 210.)

5 The *old* Count de Magpyr, in *Carpe Jugulum*.

6 Jack Frost, extending his range of ice patterns on windows in *Hogfather*.

7 The duck-billed platypus of XXXX, it would appear from certain scenes in *The Last Continent*. 'Now you've given it three legs!'

8 Leonard of Quirm, by means of a cunning artifice described in *Jingo*.

9 The replica Scone of Stone, in *The Fifth Elephant*.

10 In Angua's room at Mrs Cake's lodging house – either location is sufficient answer. (*Men at Arms*)

Guild of Interpreters III

Questions on page 84

1 'Town Hall.' Malefactors in Ankh-Morpork are not hung up by the Town Hall because there isn't one. (*Feet of Clay*)

2 The Agatean exclamation mark. (*Interesting Times*)

3 Apparently an allusion to the Internet IMHO, standing for In My Humble Opinion and generally used without visible humility. (*Carpe Jugulum*)

4 By analogy with the *Malleus Maleficarum* or Hammer of Witches, this book (cited in *Carpe Jugulum*) would appear to be the Monkey Wrench of Witches. **Bonus question:** the whole collection of related works on witch-hunting is known as the *Arca Instrumentorum* – meaning what? (See Extra Answers, page 210.)

5 Hair of the Dog. (*The Truth*)

6 Corporal Littlebottom of the Watch has the dwarfish name *Sh'rt'azs*, literally Smallbottom but sounding rather like an English term. (*Feet of Clay*)

7 'You get what you grab' is Vimes's translation of this important tenet of ownership law in *Jingo*.

8 'Mud mousse in a basket of shoe pastry,' according to the ingredient-challenged restaurant manager in *Hogfather*.

9 'One, two, THREE!' – echoing the northern English shepherds' dialect whose counting numbers begin: 'yan, tan, tethera, pethera, pimp, sethera, lethera, hovera, bovera, dick.' (*Carpe Jugulum*)

10 'I say, I say, I say.' Motto of the Fools' Guild.

11 '2 × 2' . . . as set up for the computer Hex in *Soul Music*.

12 'Untranslatable' is an acceptable answer, as is the speaker Cheery Littlebottom's comment: 'I'm afraid I can't explain in any case.' (*The Fifth Elephant*)

The Opera House

Questions on page 85

1 *The Barber of Pseudopolis* ... from our world's *The Barber of Seville*. Half a mark here, and likewise for other answers below, if you could manage only one of the two names requested. All titles except one are from *Maskerade*.

2 *Cosi fan Hita*, an awful appliance pun, from *Cosi fan Tutte*.

3 *Die Flederleiv*, from *Die Fledermaus*.

4 *Die Meistersinger von Scrote*, from *Die Meistersinger von Nürnberg*.

5 *The Enchanted Piccolo*, from *The Magic Flute*.

6 *Il Truccatore*, from *Il Trovatore*. **Bonus question:** what joke lurks in the Discworld opera's subtitle *The Master of Disguise*? (See Extra Answers, page 210.)

7 *Lohenshaak*, from *Lohengrin*.

8 *Miserable Les*, from *Les Miserables*.

9 *The Student Horse*, very merry and heavy on the quaffing, from *The Student Prince*. (*Carpe Jugulum*)

10 *La Triviata*, from *La Traviata*.

Thieves' Guild II

Questions on page 86

1 Their official cards or licences. Unlicensed thieves are frowned on, which is only the beginning of their troubles. (*Feet of Clay*)

2 Enrico Basilica, the celebrated opera tenor in *Maskerade*. **Bonus question:** what was his birth name? (See Extra Answers, page 210.)

3 Teppic the student Assassin in *Pyramids*.

4 Mr Pin, in *The Truth*. The rest of the organization consisted of Mr Tulip.

5 Nanny Ogg, in *Maskerade*. 'It wasn't theft if an Ogg was doing it.'

6 Iago, the villain of *Othello*. 'Who steals my purse steals trash . . .' and losing your reputation is much worse than losing cash. The idea of Nobby having a reputation to lose is striking.

7 Here'n'Now speaks like the narrator(s) of Damon Runyon's crime stories, told in a dialect without a past tense. One of them became a famous musical – but that's another question in another section.

8 By dragon fire, in *Guards! Guards!* Even Death conceded this was EXTREMELY UNUSUAL, CERTAINLY.

9 The stealing of the entire Agatean Empire in *Interesting Times*.

10 Here'n'Now, possibly the worst thief in the world. He thought the secret of fire might, by now, have antique value. (*Men at Arms*)

Guild of Towncriers

Questions on page 87

1 Winston Churchill on Russia: 'It is a riddle wrapped in a mystery inside an enigma . . .'

2 J. M. Barrie, *Peter Pan.* 'Second to the right and then straight on till morning.' (*The Last Hero*) **Bonus question:** why did Carrot misquote this as 'second star to the left . . .'? (See Extra Answers, page 210.)

3 Oscar Wilde, *Lady Windermere's Fan.* 'We are all in the gutter, but some of us are looking at the stars.' (*Feet of Clay*)

4 The famous 1897 editorial in *The New York Sun*, much reprinted ever since: 'Yes, Virginia, there is a Santa Claus . . .' (*Hogfather*)

5 Bram Stoker, *Dracula.* As wolves howl, Dracula says, 'Listen to them – the children of the night. What music they make!' (*The Fifth Elephant*)

6 The movie *Robocop*, alluded to more than once in *Feet of Clay*.

7 Emile Coué, French psychotherapist, suggested in 1920 that practically anything could be cured by the auto-suggestion of repeating to oneself, day in, day out: 'Every day, and in every way, I am becoming better and better.' (*Carpe Jugulum*)

8 Lord Baden-Powell, *The Wolf Cub's Handbook.* Cub Scouts would respond to 'Dyb dyb dyb' (Do Your Best) by chorusing that they will 'Dob dob dob' (Do Our Best); this embarrassing ritual was eventually abolished. In Carrot's Ankh-Morpork version, the cue and response are 'Wib wib wib' and 'Wob wob wob'.

9 The 1970s TV series *The Six Million Dollar Man*, whose hero Steve Austin is reconstructed as a superpowered cyborg: 'We can rebuild him. We have the technology.'

10 William Shakespeare, *A Midsummer Night's Dream*. Oberon: 'Ill met by moonlight, proud Titania.' (*Lords and Ladies*)

Minor Guilds
and Societies III

Questions on page 88

1 The Elucidated Brethren of the Ebon Night, in *Guards! Guards!*

2 Clockson. (*Thief of Time*)

3 The politely revolutionary Red Army in the Agatean Empire. (*Interesting Times*)

4 Corporal Nobbs of the Watch. (*Guards! Guards!*)

5 The Guild of Ratcatchers. (*Maskerade*) **Bonus question:** what was the posthumous fate of Mr Pounder, winner of the Golden Mallet for five years running? (See Extra Answers, page 211.)

6 The Cavern Club, as opposed to The Cavern, is a kind of Kennel Club for breeders of swamp dragons. (*Guards! Guards!*)

7 The poet Samuel Taylor Coleridge (*The Ancient Mariner* etc) madly joined the British army as Silas T. Cumberbatch, or Comberbache.

8 The Balancing Monks, who believe it their duty to keep the Discworld properly balanced. So far, it seems to have worked.

9 The Launderers, led at that time by Mrs Manger.

10 The Alchemists' Guild – where he picked up useful experience with firecrackers. (*Interesting Times*)

Philosophers' Tavern III

Questions on page 89

1 'Give a man a fire and he's warm for a day, but set him on fire and he's warm for the rest of his life.' (*Jingo*)

2 'If the Prophet Ossory won't go to the mountain, the mountain must go to the Prophet Ossory.' (*The Last Continent*)

3 '*Now* we're cooking with charcoal.' This variant of 'cooking with gas' appears more than once in the Discworld saga; Rincewind, for example, uses it in *Interesting Times*.

4 'Never trust a wizard over sixty-five.' Happily the current senior wizards of Unseen University had realized this to be incorrect – by a strange coincidence, at about the time they turned sixty-five. (*The Last Continent*)

5 'Walk a mile on these paws,' says Angua the werewolf bitterly. (*Jingo*)

6 '. . . we shall not lie back and let the grass grow over our heads.' A turn of phrase calculated to appeal to Campaign for Dead Rights members. (*Reaper Man*)

7 'Survival of the fastest.' Ridcully's maxim has a certain logic that would appeal to Rincewind. (*The Last Continent*) **Bonus question:** in his bath, Ridcully is offered a seasonal rendition of 'The Bells of St XXXX's' – which saint? (See Extra Answers, page 211.)

8 '. . . the Clam before the Storm.' Carrott's spelling is as legendary as his, punctuation. (*Jingo*)

9 'Been there, done that, bought the doublet . . .' (*The Fifth Elephant*)

10 '. . . take time by the foreskin.' That's Nanny Ogg for you. (*Carpe Jugulum*)

The History Monks

Questions on page 90

1 Dios, High Priest of the Sun in the land of Djelibeybi. (*Pyramids*)

2 Silver mining was prohibited, and likewise garlic cultivation, as part of the dwarfs', werewolves' and vampires' agreement at the Diet of Bugs. (*The Fifth Elephant*)

3 The secret of rock. (*Moving Pictures*) **Bonus question:** what was, in fact, the secret of rock? (See Extra Answers, page 211.)

4 The ancient Via Cloaca or municipal sewer of Ankh-Morpork, rediscovered by Watchmen Cuddy and Detritus. (*Men at Arms*)

5 The creation of the Universe, in *Eric*. The creator felt that his Big Bang 'could just as easily have been a Big Hiss, or a bit of music'. For the latter theory, see *Soul Music. . . .*

6 A meteor that long ago smashed into Copperhead Mountain in Lancre, and proved to be made of highly magnetized iron. (*Lords and Ladies*)

7 Offler, the relevant text being the *Apocrypha* to the *Vengeful Testament of Offler*. (*Feet of Clay*)

8 Alberto Malich the Wise. 'Albert' is a sufficient answer. (*Mort*)

9 Dwarfs versus trolls. It still rankled, even at the end of the Century of the Fruitbat, that the other side had laid a treacherous ambush. *Both* other sides. (*Men at Arms*)

10 In the valley of the monastery of Oi Dong, home of the Order of Wen, usually known as the History Monks. (*Thief of Time*)

The Last Order,
or The Other Order

Questions on page 91

1 *Jingo*, the novel which features *The Prid of Ankh-Morpork*, also has a ship called the *Milka* – associated with Columbus's *Pinta* through the British Milk Marketing Board slogan 'Drinka pinta milka day' (launched 1959, still remembered).

2 It's an old gag among medical students. Little William Rubin is Billy Rubin or bilirubin, a pigment formed by the breakdown of haemoglobin and largely responsible for the colour of one's Number Twos. Pratchett: 'Every batch of medical students learns it anew and Mr Rubin's name turns up in various places to general sniggering.'

3 *Soul Music*, published two years before the idea was developed at length in *Hogfather*.

4 John Milton, in *Lycidas*: 'But that two-handed engine at the door/Stands ready to smite once, and smite no more.'

5 Brewer's *Dictionary of Phrase and Fable*, originally compiled by the Rev. Ebenezer Cobham Brewer.

6 Wee Mad Arthur in *Feet of Clay* – anticipating the *other* King of the Golden River in *The Truth*.

7 Opera background for *Maskerade*, as recorded in that book's dedication. They 'showed me that opera was stranger than I could imagine'.

8 The Ancient and Truly Original Sages of the Unbroken Circle. (*The Light Fantastic*)

9 In the Corgi edition (only) of Neil Gaiman's and Terry Pratchett's *Good Omens*, a reference to the personified Famine's name changed from 'one word, six letters' to 'one word, seven letters'. Terry: 'No one knows why.' **Bonus**

question: in which *Discworld* novel was 'famine' a seven-letter word? (See Extra Answers, page 211.)

10 The Bursar of Unseen University, in *The Truth*. According to Discworld 'beta readers' he was called Worblehat 'with an O' in early drafts. Then, presumably, someone remembered his different surname in *Hogfather* ... but the 'with an O' remained. (See also 'Unseen University – The Hoodwinkers', page 18.)

11 A small New Zealand night-owl also known as the ruru or morepork. There is *no* bonus mark for fathoming its relevance to Discworld.

12 A turtle. To be precise: a species of leatherback turtle, forty million years extinct, whose bones were found in New Zealand in 1995. Its discoverer Richard Köhler named it after a favourite author called, um, wossname, hang on there, it's on the tip of my tongue ...

Extra Answers

Extra Answer: Guild of Fools and Joculators

The answer is number 6. The Foolish answers to the Fool's Guild questions are from the following sources. 1 to 4: 'Savonarola', Max Beerbohm's classic Shakespeare parody. 5: 'So That's the Way You Like It', the Shakespearean spoof from *Beyond the Fringe* by Alan Bennett, Peter Cook, Jonathan Miller and Dudley Moore. 6: *Wyrd Sisters*, the one genuine Discworld quotation from a Discworld fool. The rest are Shakespeare himself . . . 7: *Twelfth Night.* 8: *Love's Labour's Lost.* 9: *King Lear.* 10: *All's Well That Ends Well.*

Extra Answer: The Lancre Witches

Nanny Ogg . . . not Granny Weatherwax, who was indeed invited to be godmother but didn't make it to the Naming ceremony. (*Carpe Jugulum*)

Extra Answer: Offler's League of Temperance
The Green Billet, named for the wizard Drum Billet who appears in *Equal Rites* and was reincarnated as an apple tree.

Extra Answer: Guild of Engravers

The New York General Post Office building, quoting from Herodotus: 'Neither snow nor rain nor heat nor gloom of night stay these couriers from the swift completion of their appointed rounds.'

Extra Answer: Minor Guilds and Societies

'Sounds like surgery,' is what Nobby uneasily felt about the 'Colon! Out' chant.

Extra Answer: The Librarians of Time and Space

The famed Roundworld singer whose surname was borrowed

for the Melba-like prima donna of XXXX in *The Last Continent* was Dame Clara Butt.

Extra Answer: Ankh-Morpork City Watch

Dibbler had advised that you should keep the privy lid closed in case the Dragon of Unhappiness flies up your bottom.

Extra Answer: Philosophers' Tavern

Dragons. In Terry Pratchett's own words: 'The reality meter in *Moving Pictures* is loosely based on a Han dynasty (2nd Century AD) seismograph; a pendulum inside the vase moves and causes one of eight dragons to spit a ball in the direction of the tremor.'

Extra Answer: Guild of Interpreters

'No bloody women.' A regrettable policy of many ancient universities over the centuries.

Extra Answer: The Hoodwinkers

The Hero With a Thousand Faces (1949) was written by Joseph Campbell. Understandably, he failed to imagine a hero or non-hero quite like Rincewind.

Extra Answer: Guild of Teachers

Sacrephobia, a traditional problem of vampires.

Extra Answer: Guild of Actors and Mummers

The chief beggar's velvet gown comes from an old nursery rhyme. Carrot quotes the second half of the following version as the dress code of the Beggars' Guild:

Hark! Hark! The dogs do bark,
The beggars are coming to town;
Some in rags, some in tags,
And one in a velvet gown.

Extra Answer: Guild of Merchants and Traders

The droppings, muck, turds or excreta of dogs – lyrically compared by Harry King to squishy diamonds, in value if not appearance.

Extra Answer: The Order of Midnight

It was Archchancellor Mustrum Ridcully himself who (explaining that the wizards' rule about not using magic against civilians was 'more a guideline') made effective use of Stacklady's Morphic Resonator.

Extra Answer: Guild of Musicians

Lord Vetinari in *Soul Music*.

Extra Answer: Thieves' Guild

The dead thief swinging in the wind on top of the Guild building had been one who stole without a Guild licence – a salutary warning to others.

Extra Answer: Guild of Accountants

Brindisi appears to be the modern Italy of Discworld and therefore does transactions in lire. (*Unseen University Diary 1998*)

Extra Answer: Vitoller's Men

The Bearpit, mentioned in *Lords and Ladies*. According to the *Unseen University Diary 1998* it's the Bear Pit. We won't quibble.

Extra Answer: Embalmers' Guild

The last words uttered by astronaut David Bowman before entering the Star Gate in Arthur C. Clarke's novel *2001: A Space Odyssey* are, 'oh my God, *it's full of stars!*'

Extra Answer: Country Landowners' Association

The Sinking Land is a feature of Nehwon, the world of Fritz Leiber's sword-and-sorcery heroes Fafhrd and the Gray Mouser – echoed by the similar duo Bravd and the Weasel in *The Colour of Magic*.

Extra Answer: Guild of Alchemists

Granny Weatherwax showed off with these pyrotechnics at the Lancre Witch Trials in 'The Sea and Little Fishes'.

Extra Answer: Assassins' Guild

The one-of-a-kind which the Patrician couldn't bear to destroy was Leonard of Quirm, inventor of the gonne and much other dread weaponry – all in a spirit of pure innocence and the belief that no one could ever use such devices in battle.

Extra Answer: Guild of Haberdashers

Ankhstones are logically explained by a footnote in *Sourcery*: 'Like rhinestones, but different river.'

Extra Answer: Guild of Apothecaries

In the troll tipple 'molten sulphur on coke with phosphoric acid', the last ingredient actually is an ingredient of Coke (as in Coca-Cola).

Extra Answer: Guild of Actors and Mummers II

The Story of Ook. It would be tempting to link the Librarian's title with that celebrated French pornographic work *The Story of O*, but even quizmasters draw the line somewhere.

Extra Answer: Guild of Engravers II

The little brass lever marked 'Organ Interlock'. Better not to ask, really, but it gets pulled a few pages from the end of *Hogfather*. Have a mark anyway if you named the other lever that also has to be pulled before disaster, 'Musical Pipes'.

Extra Answer: Mrs Widgery's Lodgers

The Bursar hallucinated that he could fly, and since he *was* a wizard his 'hallucinations' were effective enough to fool gravity and generate UFO reports. (*The Truth*)

Extra Answer: Guild of Seamstresses

Carrot ordered *The Perfumed Allotment* in the course of educating himself about Klatch, expecting it to be full of cultural insight from the nation that invented gardens.

Extra Answer: The Librarians of Time and Space II

The question, asked by book dealer 'ppint', was approximately 'What does the Tooth Fairy *do* with all those teeth?'

Extra Answer: Guild of Cooks and Chefs

The Stone of Scone is now in Edinburgh Castle, having been restored to Scotland in 1997 after some 700 years in English hands. So no marks for the outdated answer 'under the royal Coronation Chair in London'.

Extra Answer: Guild of Engravers III

BBC Radio's *Desert Island Discs*, in which celebrities are asked what eight favourite music recordings, plus one luxury item, they'd take to a desert island. Terry Pratchett was a *Desert Island Discs* guest in 1997, and as his luxury item chose the Chrysler Building.

Extra Answer: Minor Guilds and Societies II

The newspaper's original intended title was *Ankh-Morpork Items*.

Extra Answer: The Venerable Council of Seers

The Enigma machine was used for cipher communications by Nazi Germany during World War II, and its encryption was famously broken by a team of experts (including Alan Turing) and a primitive computer at Bletchley Park in England.

Extra Answer: Campaign for Equal Heights

The Harvard Lampoon's raucous Tolkien spoof *Bored of the Rings* (by Henry N. Beard and Douglas C. Kenny, 1968) parodies the original Gimli, son of Gloin, with Gimlet, son of Groin.

Extra Answer: The Librarians of Time and Space III

Just common sense, really: 'Use more than eighty virgins and even quite a large bath will overflow . . .' It would appear that Vlad's sister Lacrimosa has made the experiment.

Extra Answer: Guild of Cunning Artificers

First, the flush toilet in its modern form was marketed and popularized in Victorian times by the all too appropriately named Thomas Crapper. Second, Sir Charles Lavatory's title is surely a nod to the original Elizabethan inventor of the flush toilet, Sir John Harington. (A mark for either answer.) Note that lavatories have been called both crappers and johns. . . .

Extra Answer: Guild of Shoemakers and Leatherworkers

Vimes hated the injustice that a man who could afford fifty-dollar boots would have the same good boots and dry feet in ten years' time, while others could spend a hundred dollars on cheap boots over the years and still have wet feet. Poverty comes expensive.

Extra Answer: Priests', Sacerdotes' and Occult Intermediaries' Guild

A small black bean. Discworld legends mentioned in *Hogfather* incorporate both the traditional Bean-King game (whoever gets the Twelfth Night cake with the bean in it is jokily treated as king for a day) and the darker legend of the Year King, chosen to reign for a year before being sacrificed.

Extra Answer: Guild of Tailors

Edgar Allan Poe's 'The Masque of the Red Death'.

Extra Answer: Ankh-Morpork City Watch II

Walago is 'A kind of pastry made from curtains'. (*The Fifth Elephant*)

Extra Answer: Guild of Haberdashers II

Surely a nod to the late Rod Hull and his popular hand-and-arm puppet 'Emu', frequently seen on British TV in the 1970s. Emu didn't look much like an emu, but closely resembled the description of the falconer's garish 'glove'.

Extra Answer: Guild of Gamblers

999,943 to one. (*Guards! Guards!*) Oh, all right, have half a mark if you said anything *less than* a million to one.

Extra Answer: The Librarians of Time and Space IV

The Man in the Moone, the 1638 novel of bird-powered spaceflight, was written by Bishop Francis Godwin. If you guessed Anonymous, have a mark anyway – it was indeed published anonymously after Godwin's death.

Extra Answer: College of Heralds

Ridcully had incautiously declared that a little bit of planetary engineering work would soon be carried out, 'or my name's not Mustrum Ridcully . . .' Later in the same book he tempted fate again by saying, 'And, while you can call me Mr Silly –'

Extra Answer: Philosophers' Tavern II

'I never drink . . . wine,' as Dracula – played by Bela Lugosi – says meaningfully in the 1931 *Dracula* movie directed by Tod Browning. Francis Ford Coppola's 1992 *Bram Stoker's Dracula* echoed this classic line by way of homage.

Extra Answer: Guild of Interpreters II

A tautology.

Extra Answer: Guild of Lawyers

'Do not act incautiously when confronting little bald wrinkly smiling men!' Men, that is, like Lu Tze.

Extra Answer: Guild of Actors and Mummers III

Oscar Wilde's *The Importance of Being Earnest*, in which hero Jack Worthing was once a foundling abandoned (or at any rate mislaid) in a handbag.

Extra Answer: Guild of Merchants and Traders II

The great and malodorous city of Ankh-Morpork is the Great Wahoonie, just as New York is the Big Apple.

Extra Answer: Cable Street Particulars

Unadorned Facts is the Discworld analogue of the Worldwide Church of God's fundamentalist magazine The Plain Truth (founded by the late Herbert W. Armstrong).

Extra Answer: Guild of Fools and Joculators II

Bjorn Again is or was an Australian band that concentrated exclusively on cover versions of Abba songs.

Extra Answer: Guild of Apothecaries II

Bursar Disease, named for that university official. Someone whom we might call dippy, dotty or doolally is, in the evolving vernacular of Ankh-Morpork, a little bit (or a lot) bursar.

Extra Answer: Guild of Engravers and Printers

Six years before his starring role in an actual novel, William de Worde featured in the 1994 first edition of *The Discworld Companion*, which prophetically remarked: 'It could well be that the future holds great things for young de Worde. . . .'

Extra Answer: Campaign for Dead Rights

The Street of Small Gods and Broad Way. Allow yourself half a mark if you got only one.

Extra Answer: Guild of Accountants II

The gangs were called the Skats and the Mohocks. Have a full point even if you could name only one.

Extra Answer: Silicon Anti-Defamation League

The alleged Troll Tooth Fairy called himself Clinkerbell.

Extra Answer: The Sages of the Unknown Shadow

B.El.L. Bachelor of Eldritch Lacemaking. This degree has never been satisfactorily explained. (*The Discworld Companion*)

Extra Answer: Strippers' Guild

President for Life of the Guild – and, indeed, the entire committee. (*The Discworld Companion*)

Extra Answer: Guild of Armourers

The gods seems to be playing the board game Cluedo (in America, Clue). 'I accuse the Reverend Green in the library with the candlestick . . .' or with the rope, the revolver, etc. The double-handed axe, however, is not an available Cluedo weapon.

Extra Answer: College of Heralds II

The robber crab, a land crab from the southwest Pacific region which prefers to live in burrows but does indeed climb trees.

Extra Answer: Guild of Architects

The Djinn Palace. (*Pyramids*)

Extra Answer: Guild of Musicians II

Lady Sybil Ramkin.

Extra Answer: Smugglers' Guild

Stoolie is both a gnoll with literal plants growing on him, and a police informer or grass – doubly representing that favourite focus of JFK conspiracy theorists, the Grassy Knoll.

Extra Answer: Guild of Cunning Artificers II

Lobster.

Extra Answer: Beggars' Guild

According to Terry Pratchett, 'Millennium hand and shrimp' popped out when he fed various texts into the program Babble, which blends its sources into a kind of prose remix. The shrimp can be traced to a Chinese menu he used; the 'millennium hand' quite probably came from 'Particle Man', a song by They Might Be Giants (a group our author likes) that becomes lyrical about a watch with a millennium hand and eon hand.

Extra Answer: Ankh-Morpork City Watch III

It's likely that 'Bridisian' should read 'Brindisian', since Brindisi is established as a Discworld country. They eat pasta there. (*Maskerade*)

Extra Answer: Fine Art Appreciation Society

Leviathan (1651), by Thomas Hobbes.

Extra Answer: Guild of Interpreters III

Arca Instrumentorum is Chest of Tools, or maybe just toolbox.

Extra Answer: The Opera House

Truccatore is Italian for make-up artist. A related gag is that the hero of *Il Truccatore: The Master of Disguise* is also known as The Man with a Thousand Faces – a nickname of Lon Chaney, who played the Phantom of the Opera in the original silent movie production.

Extra Answer: Thieves' Guild II

Henry Slugg.

Extra Answer: Guild of Towncriers

J. M. Barrie's original line in his play and novel *Peter Pan* didn't mention a star. The Disney movie changed it to the now more familiar 'second star to the left and straight on 'til morning'.

Extra Answer: Minor Guilds and Societies III

He was reincarnated as a rat. Although he didn't believe in reincarnation, reincarnation believed in him.

Extra Answer: Philosophers' Tavern III

'The Bells of St Ungulant's.' (*Hogfather*)

Extra Answer: The History Monks

Apparently the trollish secret of rock is that you can pick one up and throw it at someone. (*The Discworld Companion*)

Extra Answer: The Last Order, or The Other Order

Maskerade, in the engravers'-office scene: we learn that Mr Cripslock will have to engrave page 11 of the Almanack again, because 'He's spelled 'famine' with seven letters –' Of course this alludes to the oddity in *Good Omens*.

Afterword

How did you do? There are 775 basic points to be scored, plus a Bonus Answer in each of the 75 quiz rounds, for a grand total of 850. If you scored more than this, you are probably a sourcerer and entitled to the supreme honorary title *Doctorum Fiddleri Tempus-Minimus*.

Otherwise, totals in the range 0–99 suggest that although you have a wonderful personality and good hair, you should read some more of that nice Mr Pratchett's books and try again. You are the Wyrdest Link. If you scored in the range 100–749, you gain honorary citizenship of that magical Discworld region from which so many over- and under-achievers come . . . you are the Wyrdest Lancre, and also win the Mrs Cake Happy Medium Award. If you managed 750 or above, you clearly share the deep learning of those revered dwarfs the *drudak'ak*.*
You have ripped through this quizbook like a deadly predator, the Wyrdest Lynx.

A few final notes . . .

Virtually all the Guilds, societies and other groups used for quiz titles in *The Wyrdest Link* are lifted straight from Discworld stories, where new ones continue to emerge and old ones acquire names at last. For example, the Guild of Accountants appears in *Jingo*, the Guild of Architects in *The Truth* and the Guild of Cunning Artificers not until *The Last Hero* – although Terry Pratchett said when quizzed, 'I've always assumed that they existed!' (There has long been a Street of Cunning Artificers in Ankh-Morpork.)

I took the liberty of extending Actors to Actors and Mummers because it sounded nicer, and of inventing – or at least prematurely naming – the Guilds of Apothecaries, Cooks & Chefs, and Interpreters. Surely they must exist . . . like the Guild of Armourers, which I thought I'd made up and then found lurking in *Jingo*.

Meanwhile, the enciphered message in this book's copyright

---

* Translated in *The Fifth Elephant* as 'They do not get out in the fresh air enough.'

page reads as follows: 'David Langford has served well in the worldwide Conspiracy's cover-up of UFOs, Alien Grays, Bigfoot and Elvis sightings, and the British royal family's secret identities as giant vampire lizards. Loyal worker Langford is due $5,000,000 in back payments from CIA funds.' It seems worth a try.

Again, thanks to Terry Pratchett for writing the novels which made all this possible, for his patience in allowing a second quizbook in the wake of *The Unseen University Challenge*, and his insane generosity in contributing a *third* introduction to a Langford volume. Others associated with the irresistible juggernaut of Discworld are too numerous to list, but I'm especially grateful to alt.fan.pratchett, Leo Breebaart, Stephen Briggs and Jo Fletcher of Gollancz, Josh Kirby, Colin Smythe, and www.lspace.org. My fervent thanks go to Colette Reap of the fascinating earrings, and Alan Bellingham, who kindly acted as beta readers. My heroic literary agent Christopher Priest offered much valuable advice beginning with, 'Hadn't you better start writing that bloody book?'

A final thank-you to two whole Discworld-loving countries for hospitality and much-appreciated free trips overseas. Finland, and in particular the Jyväskylä SF Club 42, entertained me splendidly as a guest of Finncon in 2001. Australia, and in particular the SF fans of Adelaide and Melbourne, gave me equally lavish treatment on the occasion of the World SF Convention down under in 1999. I even met some guy called Terry Pratchett there. He did not have corks around his hat.

David Langford, October 2001
www.ansible.demon.co.uk

If you've turned to the back of the book looking for the **Answers**, they begin on page 93 and the **Extra Answers** begin on page 197.